STARTING WITH DESCAR

Continuum's *Starting with . . .* series offers clear, concise and access-ible introductions to the key thinkers in philosophy. The books explore and illuminate the roots of each philosopher's work and ideas, leading readers to a thorough understanding of the key influ-ences and philosophical foundations from which his or her thought developed. Ideal for first-year students starting out in philosophy, the series will serve as the ideal companion to study of this fascinat-ing subject.

Available now:

Starting with Derrida, Sean Gaston

Starting with Nietzsche, Ullrich Haase

Forthcoming:

Starting with Berkeley, Nick Jones

Starting with Hegel, Craig B. Matarrese

Starting with Heidegger, Thomas Greaves

Starting with Hobbes, George Macdonald Ross

Starting with Hume, Charlotte R. Brown and William Edward Morris

Starting with Kant, Andrew Ward

Starting with Leibniz, Lloyd Strickland

Starting with Mill, John R. Fitzpatrick

Starting with Rousseau, James Delaney

Starting with Wittgenstein, Chon Tejedor

STARTING WITH DESCARTES

C. G. PRADO

continuum

Continuum International Publishing Group
The Tower Building   80 Maiden Lane
11 York Road   Suite 704
London SE1 7NX   New York, NY 10038

www.continuumbooks.com

© C.G. Prado 2009

British Library Cataloguing-in-Publication Data
A catalogue record for this book is available from the British Library.

ISBN: HB: 978-0-8264-4609-1
PB: 978-0-8264-3664-1

Library of Congress Cataloging-in-Publication Data
Prado, C. G.
Starting with Descartes / C. G. Prado.
p. cm.
Includes bibliographical references and index.
1. Descartes, René, 1596–1650. Meditationes de prima philosophia.
2. First philosophy.   I. Title.
B1854.P733 2009
194—dc22
2008048189

Typeset by RefineCatch Limited, Bungay, Suffolk
Printed and bound in Great Britain by
MPG Books Ltd, Bodmin, Cornwall

CONTENTS

CONTENTS

CHAPTER 1

INTRODUCTION

This book is about one man's quest, a quest that Plato (428–348 BCE) saw as a sacred mission and Friedrich Nietzsche (1844–1900) saw as a malignant obsession. The man was René Descartes (1596–1650) and his quest was for absolute truth and unconditional knowledge. This book also is about how Descartes, often called 'the Father of Modern Philosophy,' determined that epistemological issues – questions about truth and knowledge (see Glossary) – would dominate philosophical thinking for more than 300 years after his own time.

Attitudes toward truth and knowledge have changed in crucial ways in the historically recent past. Nietzsche's rejection of conception of truth as absolute enabled questions to be raised about the nature of truth and thinkers he influenced challenged, if not usurped, the dominance of thinkers who owed their allegiance to Plato and Descartes and held truth absolute. But if you want to understand philosophy in the tradition established by the ancient Greeks and continued by Western Europeans and North Americans, you need to understand Descartes' thinking about truth and knowledge, how he thought they were wholly objective, how he thought reason made them attainable, and the problems generated by his objectives, assumptions, and methods.

* * *

There have been many intellectually and historically pivotal philosophers, beginning with Socrates (469–399 BCE), Plato, and Aristotle (384–322 BCE), but if you were faced with the choice of mastering the works of just two of them in order to understand Anglo-European philosophy, especially epistemology or the theory of knowledge, then Descartes' *Meditations on First Philosophy*, published in 1641, would be one of the two works. The other would be the *Critique of Pure Reason*, published in 1781 by Immanuel Kant (1724–1804).

I mention the *Critique*, not only to note its importance, but also to indicate a contrast that you need to appreciate from the beginning. The *Critique* is a very difficult book, but its difficulty is evident to its readers. A serious problem posed by the *Meditations* is that they do not seem to be particularly difficult, and too often are read superficially and so not properly understood. As you will soon learn, there is much in Descartes' meditations that is centrally important but is tacit, presumed, implied, or in some cases somewhat disingenuous. The *Meditations*, then, require as careful reading as does the *Critique*.

It is unfortunate that Descartes' six meditations are deceptively easy; they are a popular introductory text but invite serious interpretive problems that sometimes thwart the introductory purpose they are supposed to serve. I warn you about the danger of not reading the *Meditations* carefully and probingly, not only to help you understand Descartes' position and arguments, but to alert you to how you need to read philosophy. Regardless of texts' initial appearances, you need to identify assumptions and presuppositions, to recognize circular or otherwise faulty argument, and to grasp when key ideas and concepts are being only implicitly introduced or altered.

What makes reading the *Meditations* tricky is that they can be – and usually are – read with little or no recognition of what Descartes assumes and presupposes, of how he changes philosophical concepts by arguing as he does, of how he introduces problematic notions while appearing to be using familiar ones. The deceptive appearance of the *Meditations* is why books about them – including this one – are inevitably longer than the *Meditations* themselves. Regardless of appearances, though, the *Meditations*, like the *Critique*, are philosophy at its purest and most abstract, and mastering the *Meditations* initiates you into a kind and level of thinking very few ever achieve or appreciate. In the end, and despite the difficulties, mastering Descartes' *Meditations* will prove less a daunting task than an intellectual adventure.

* * *

My main objective in this book is to help you to understand the arguments of the *Meditations*, to appreciate their implications, to show you the errors and infelicities they incorporate, and in doing so to contribute to your introduction to philosophy. As noted, the *Meditations*, more a pamphlet than a book when compared to other philosophy texts, present special interpretive problems. Descartes' six meditations are laden with conceptual assumptions and even circular thinking and someone not already familiar with philosophy runs the risk of being seriously misled by them. Unfortunately, the *Meditations* not only appear deceptively straightforward, they often are taught as if they are more straightforward than in fact they are. A former student of mine once talked about her introductory philosophy course with a friend from another university. After she described what we were doing with the *Meditations*, her friend told her to be leery of her professor – me – because there just was not that much in Descartes' little book!

Misinterpretation of the *Meditations* is not only the fault of their readers and teachers but also of their author. It was essential to Descartes' intentions that the six meditations be read by people as if they were themselves doing the meditating, the aim being that the contentions made in each of the meditations be appropriated by their readers. To this end Descartes wrote with a certain facility that assumed the intuitive clarity of what he had to say. One source of the interpretive problems, therefore, is that while Descartes saw himself as offering clear and accessible arguments that he was convinced would be self-evident to anyone who read them with an open mind, those arguments involved problematic assumptions and novel uses of familiar concepts. Despite Descartes' best efforts, the six meditations contain circularities and unargued-for suppositions. The most central of the latter are Descartes' understandings of the nature of the self and of consciousness or awareness, and as you will see hereafter, both are understandings with highly dubious implications.

Your task is a compound one: you have to read each meditation as if it were your own, but at the same time you have to probe and assess, question and test the very things you supposedly are thinking through. And since much of the content of the *Meditations* has to do with critical analysis and evaluation, you have to analyze the analyses and evaluate the evaluations – tasks you will grow familiar with as you progress in your study of philosophy.

* * *

To proceed, I need to introduce a number of points in order to provide a foundation for discussion of Descartes and the *Meditations*. These are points about language, about reason and truth, about what exists, about the historical context of Descartes' work, about reactions to his work, about the discipline of philosophy, and about some practical matters. Most of the various points will be followed up in subsequent chapters, but all need to be made here to give you some touchstones before we begin discussing the *Meditations*, as well as an idea of the sort of issues you will be dealing with as we continue with this introduction to Descartes. You probably will feel some frustration and perhaps a little lost as you read through the balance of this chapter, but if you persevere the several points will become clear and you will get that much more out of the chapters on the *Meditations* and out of the *Meditations* themselves.

PRELIMINARY REMARKS

1 Language

Alfred North Whitehead (1861–1947) once described philosophy as a series of footnotes to Plato. Like many famous and often-quoted remarks, this comment captures a significant truth, but it obscures a fundamental change in philosophical thinking initiated by Descartes. As indicated earlier, Descartes changed some key philosophical concepts, such as that of the self and of consciousness, and I will have more to say about them hereafter, but the change I want to highlight here is special in that Descartes most likely was unaware of making it, despite its centrality to his thought. The change has to do with language, and therefore with how truth's nature is conceived, but it also affects his conceptions of consciousness and the self. The point is of some difficulty for novices, and raising it this early on is a bit risky as it likely will not make a lot of sense to you until you have read more. However, this is a point that needs to be introduced early for three reasons.

The first reason is that in order for you to learn to read and do philosophy, you need to distance yourself from language a little and that can begin with consideration of how Descartes used language in a new way. The second reason is that the change was of great importance to how some responded to Descartes' work. The third is the most significant reason, and is that the change was at once part of how Descartes reconceived the self and consciousness, and part of what enabled those reconceptions. In this way, the change illustrates something Descartes failed to see: that language shapes thought as much as thought shapes language.

The change in language, or better, in how language is thought of, was best articulated by a postmodern (see Glossary) philosopher who rejected Descartes' absolutist conceptions of truth and knowledge in favor of truth and knowledge as relative to temporally and contextually circumscribed linguistic practices, and whose methods and objectives owed more to Nietzsche than to Plato or Descartes (Prado 2000). In *The Order of Things*, Michel Foucault (1926–1984) distinguished between 'trinary' and 'binary' conceptions of language (Foucault 1973, 60). His point was that prior to Descartes, words or 'signs' were generally conceived as meaningful, as connected to the things they referred to or signified, because of a relation of 'natural resemblance.' This meant that there were three things involved in the meaningfulness of words: the word or sign, the thing signified, and a natural resemblance that associated the word or sign with the thing referred to or signified. This is why Foucault calls the conception 'trinary.' Though it is not very clear just what the natural resemblance consisted of, the basic notion was that words meant what they did because they bore a certain similitude to what they stood for or named due to all things being products of divine creation.

When Descartes isolated consciousness in a way we will consider hereafter, words were recast as being arbitrarily assigned to what they stood for or named; there ceased to be any supposed connecting similitude that made meaningfulness possible. Instead there came to be only two factors involved in meaningfulness: words or signs and what they were used to refer to or signify. This is why Foucault describes this Cartesian (the adjectival form of 'Descartes') conception as 'binary.' In this conception, what connects words to what they name or refer to is not some inherent resemblance but our decisions to use particular words to stand for particular things.

The important point here, which has major significance for what follows, is that we can and sometimes need to distance ourselves enough from language to theorize about its nature and how it works, not just practically, in the sense of studying how different natural languages compare and evolve, but fundamentally. We can theorize about what it is to have and to employ Capital-L Language in the sense of having the capacity to speak one or more natural languages. Descartes' conception was of language as little more than a kind of labeling system; language was secondary to and a product of thought, having no conditioning feedback on thought. This means that Descartes was unprepared to recognize, much less consider, how his use of language affected his conceptions, arguments, and conclusions.

Though I will not pursue the matter, I will mention as a point of contrast one historically recent and influential school of philosophy opposed to Descartes' conception of language, namely, structuralism. Structuralists, followers of linguist and semioticist Ferdinand de Saussure (1857–1913), held that language or 'discourse' is a system that importantly determines thought and the nature and content of the concepts we use. However, as noted, Descartes does not consider this point and would have categorically disagreed with it if he had.

What you need to keep in mind as we proceed is that Descartes did not reflect on language's influence on thought. As will emerge, this lack of reflection poses problems for his claims about the intuitiveness and evidency of points he makes because he fails to consider how his use of language has a tendentious impact on the framing of his arguments' premises and conclusions.

2 Reason and Truth

Descartes profoundly believed that we can reason our way to objective truth and are able to acquire timeless and certain knowledge about ourselves and the world – and to some extent about God. This was the essence of the modern philosophy Descartes fathered: truth-attaining reason displaced faith, tradition, and claimed revelation. (Note that 'modern' does not here mean current or up-to-date; 'modern' in 'modern philosophy' designates reason-centered philosophizing as initiated by Descartes.) However, nothing essential changed with respect to the conception of truth inherited from Plato; all that changed was construal of how it was attained. Like those before him, Descartes believed that truth was absolute, wholly objective, and completely independent of human interests and perspectives. Truth's discernment was in some cases dependent on historical developments, such as how much science might be known at a particular time or the level of development of disciplines like philosophy – witness Galileo's achievement and Descartes' own claimed breakthroughs – but truth itself was not dependent on historical developments.

It is in connection with truth's discernment that we find Descartes' signature operating principle: to attain truth we have to analytically parse everything we believe or are inclined to believe into its simplest component parts. We then must establish the truth of each of the components or discard them as false, and we must be relentless in doing so. Once we have only true components in hand, we reassemble them, and if we can reconstruct the original beliefs, we must accept and hold them as true; if we cannot, we must abandon the beliefs as false or alter them as necessary to make them true.

For Descartes, then, objective truth was real, absolute, and accessible, and wholly certain knowledge was not only possible, it was the proper aim of intellectual inquiry, whether it is inquiry into the nature of God, into our own nature, or into the state of the world. Descartes' view of truth had Plato as its intellectual progenitor; it was his methodology for attaining truth that was new. Where Plato relied on dialectic, Descartes put his trust in analysis.

Few contemporaries quarrel with Descartes' analytic methodology, but most have little patience with its aim as the attainment of objective truth. Many now think truth and knowledge are functions of established practices, perspectives, interests, and temporal, social, and cultural contexts. Even the 'hard' truths of the physical sciences are thought to be conditioned by attitudinal factors, witness the numerous feminist critiques of traditional scientific thinking and methods (Fox-Keller 1985). As I consider in the Conclusion, we now are closer to Nietzsche than to Descartes and think Miguel de Cervantes (1547–1616) got it right in *Don Quixote* when he described history as 'the mother of truth.'

Cervantes' remark about history captures the heart of the difference between Cartesian and Nietzschean conceptions of truth. Descartes thought truth was 'ahistorical,' unaffected by historical changes and developments. Truth was entirely independent of interpretation and of how interpretation might be influenced or determined. Contrary to this, Nietzsche had a 'historicist' understanding of truth: he thought truth to be a function of perspective and context and so a function of temporal developments. For Nietzsche, there were not facts; for him there are 'only interpretations' (Nietzsche 1968a, 267).

3 Objective/Subjective

My use of the term 'objective' to describe truth as Descartes conceived of it actually would have been confusing to him. He would not have agreed with what I say earlier because he used the term 'subjective' as I used 'objective,' referring to what we call objective as actual or formal. This use of 'objective' for 'subjective' causes much confusion for readers of the *Meditations* who are not forewarned, and it must be kept in mind as we proceed to enable the best possible understanding of Descartes' contentions.

I mention the use of 'objective' for 'subjective' not only to prevent confusion but also partly for pedagogical reasons. The reversal nicely illustrates how differences in the use of language radically affect the understanding of philosophical texts, especially those written in times earlier than our own. Imagine working your way through the *Meditations* taking each occurrence of 'objective' in the contemporary sense and not as Descartes used the term – that is, as we use 'subjective.' How could you grasp what Descartes actually meant? For instance, you would interpret his claims about the objective reality of an idea as being about its actual or external or mind-independent reality, when he would be talking about the determinateness of a mental object, of the idea as an idea. Nor are we dealing here with what many would dismiss as a pedantic point; we are dealing with a significant communications issue. As you read the *Meditations*, if when Descartes speaks of objective reality you think he meant mind-independent reality, when what he actually meant was the reality of ideas in the mind – a reality which he precisely contrasted with mind-independent reality – you will not grasp his arguments nor their implications for epistemology.

In its present sense, the term 'objective,' where it does not refer to an aim or goal, refers to what is impartial, detached, neutral, unbiased, and unprejudiced; in short, what is objective contrasts with everything that is subjective or shaped by interpretation and all the factors that determine interpretation. A judge's ruling, for instance, must be objective, and not be influenced by bias or special interests. In philosophy the term 'objective' is used to refer to what exists in the world, to existents the being or reality of which does not depend in any way on point of view or any one's experience. If we describe a truth, a fact, an event, or a thing as objective, it means that its being what it is does not depend on how it is seen or construed. When we talk about something being subjective, on the other hand, we do mean something that depends on being experienced. Strawberries exist as things in the world, regardless of whether anyone ever tastes them; but the taste of strawberries, being subjective, exists only when someone is savoring strawberries.

In Descartes' terminology 'objective' had the opposite sense to what it has now. For Descartes, 'objective' referred to the object of thought as what is thought, not to the object of thought as what is thought about. For him, what is thought about is the subject of thought, as we say that someone is the subject of a portrait. Subjects are the things in the world, what there is in reality, and which may causally produce representations of themselves as ideas with objective existence in individual minds.

4 Substances

Something's being taken as real – as objective in our sense of the term – presupposes a good deal about what it is to exist. Descartes took it as given that if they exist at all, the subjects of our thoughts and perceptions exist in their own right, independently of anything else – with the qualification that, as created things, nothing that exists is independent of God's creative and sustaining will. Descartes followed Aristotle in conceiving of existents as substances (see Glossary) with properties. Something existent is either a substance, and hence an independent being, or it is a property, and hence dependent on a substance.

Substances have properties of two sorts: defining or essential properties, and 'accidental' or nonessential properties. Substance may have numerous accidental or nonessential properties that may vary at different times and in different ways, but their essential or defining properties are what make substances what they are. The paradigm case, in Aristotle, is a person: a person is a substance, a material entity, a living creature, defined by the property of being rational. Persons may be short or tall, blue-eyed or brown-eyed, but what makes them persons is that they are rational. Descartes accepts the basic Aristotelian conception of substances and their defining properties, but as we will see in Chapter 4, he alters a key aspect because instead of conceiving of human beings as rational animals, Descartes conceives of himself, and so of other persons, as purely mental substances defined only by thought.

This last point is the main reason I here anticipate discussion of substances in Chapter 4. It is important for you to understand early on that when Descartes talks about a possibly existent entity or thing which may be an object of thought, he may be talking about one or both of two radically different kinds of things: mental things and material things. How he makes the distinction will be clarified in Chapter 4, but awareness of the mental/material distinction is crucial prior to your beginning the *Meditations* because Descartes assumes the distinction in how he sets up his methodology. If you are not forewarned, you may accept the distinction without realizing it as you follow his methodological argument – especially since the distinction will appear familiar to you.

The key point is that material substances can be objects of thought in the sense that the objective reality of the ideas we have of them is caused by their actual, in-the-world reality. Against this, mental substances, with a single exception, can be objects of thought only inferentially. The all-important exception is one's own mind, which is known directly and is the only mental substance that can be known directly. It is known directly through immediate experience of its defining property: its own thought. Other minds can be objects of thought only inferentially: we infer that there are other minds on the basis of the behavior of some material substances: physical bodies like our own that behave as we do.

5 Ahistorical/Historical Truth

To return to truth as historical and as ahistorical, you may have balked, as many do, at the idea that true statements could be true in virtue of social or cultural milieus, practices, perspectives, or interests. Consider the statement: 'Water expands when it freezes.' How could the truth of this statement be subject to historical change? If the statement were 'Water loses caloric fluid when it freezes' or 'Water loses mean kinetic energy when it freezes,' we would accept that the former was held true at one time but no longer, and that the latter is held true now. But to say that water takes up more room in a frozen state than in a liquid state surely is undeniably true at any time. Ice floats, and if you fill a bottle with water and put it in your freezer, when it freezes it will burst the bottle. 'Water expands when it freezes' surely must be ahistorically true; it must be true at any time and in any context.

However, things are more complicated than they appear. The trouble is that empirical truths (see Glossary), the truths we learn about the physical world through experience, cannot be ahistorical because such things as water expanding when it freezes are contingent. That is, these are truths dependent on physics and chemistry working as they presently work. We do not know what changes might come about that could make water contract on freezing; we do not even know if in some other galaxy water now does contract when it freezes. The same sort of point can be made about any presently true scientific statement. Things were different for Descartes. His conception of physical reality as God-created was a conception of a reality not amenable to the kinds of fundamental changes that we now can at least envisage as possible. To argue that the statement 'Water expands when it freezes' articulates an ahistorical truth, then, is to side with Descartes and accept a mid-seventeenth-century vision of physical reality as wholly and forever determined to be as it is by divine will.

To continue to defend ahistorical truth, the alternative is to focus on *a priori* truth (see Glossary), on truth that is necessary and conceptual and independent of experience, such as that the internal angles of a triangle add up to 180 degrees. The trouble with this alternative, though, is that it does not yield uncontroversial ahistorical truths that are very interesting, since they are mostly true by definition. In any case, what is and is not true *a priori* is debatable (Audi 1996, 29).

Philosophically, the view of truth as historical, as contingent on cultural or individual factors, is known as relativism (see Glossary), and there are various forms of relativism, some more radical than others (Krausz 1989). Relativism goes back much earlier than Nietzsche, most notably to Protagoras (c. 485–410 BCE), who claimed that human beings are 'the measure of all things,' that it is we who determine what is or is not true in how we perceive things to be (Matson 2000, 89). In the present context, a more useful point of departure is G. W. F. Hegel (1770–1831), who offered perhaps the most plausible basis for understanding truth as historical. This basis was Hegel's insight that any claimed truth, whether about ourselves or about the world, always is redescribable in different terms and from different perspectives. The essential point about redescription is that any statement of a claimed truth can be restated, and thus shown to be only one among various possible construals or interpretations of what is claimed to be true.

I will need to return to the issue of relativistic truth hereafter because you, as a contemporary, cannot be introduced to Descartes without acknowledgment that your intellectual context accommodates a conception of truth he utterly rejected, but a conception of truth that undoubtedly will influence your reading because of your likely greater tolerance or even endorsement of relativistic thinking. Despite that influence, you need to appreciate how Descartes' aim was to ground human knowledge on an indubitable foundation, and how he not only rejected any form of relativism, but had to do so because for him truth was absolute and the very possibility of his project and methodology required that truth be absolute.

Part of the significance of Descartes' conception of truth is that, as did many of his contemporaries, he saw a threat of relativism in the intellectual upheaval occurring in his time. Descartes did welcome the upheaval as a way of breaking with dogmatism and authoritarianism. He was enthusiastic about the challenging of established assumptions and methods of inquiry by exciting new ideas and novel perspectives, and especially by the new reliance on reason. But he thought it vital to replace authoritarianism and dogmatism with reason-discerned ahistorical truth, thinking that things would only go from bad to worse if authority and dogmatism were replaced by relativism. As I consider in the next chapter, contrary to how it is usually portrayed, Descartes' work was less a positive, participatory contribution to the innovations of his day, than a conservative response to them, witness his concern not to challenge religious doctrines and how he opens the *Meditations*.

6 Reason Ascendant

To better appreciate how Descartes saw the intellectual turmoil around him, you need to focus on the new confidence and optimism regarding our ability to reason about issues that had up to that time been considered matters of faith or unquestionable givens supported by authorities thought unimpeachable. Science, broadly speaking, was beginning to assert itself, to spill over the boundaries religion had imposed on it. The confidence and optimism in reason were supported by a nascent but increasing reliance on experimentation. Most notably, Galileo Galilei (1564–1642) revitalized the then still theoretical heliocentrism of Copernicus (1473–1543) using empirical evidence made possible by the invention of the telescope. As is well known, Galileo prompted theological authorities to protest against his work and in the end to condemn it and to demand he retract his claims. But the protest and condemnation only served to underscore the scope and importance of his challenge to orthodoxy.

What Descartes shared with those causing the intellectual upheaval was his appreciation of the power of reason. Descartes saw his predecessors and too many of his contemporaries as burdened with dogmatism, as espousing beliefs for which they had no real evidence and that were supported only by tradition and the authority of the Church. For Descartes, events taking place around him seemed to confirm how productive human reason could be freed from faith-based and doctrine-determined constraints. He felt driven to produce a new and more productive philosophical methodology, which he describes in his *Discourse on Method* (1637) and implements in the *Meditations* (1641). As we have seen, the heart of his methodology was critical analysis of concepts and beliefs. While his more empirically oriented colleagues were examining the physical world much more closely, Descartes set out to have a thorough and unstinting look at the world of ideas.

From our point of view, Descartes' zeal regarding reason may look a little naïve, but that is a perspective available to us only because of all we have learned since his time. He looks to have been too innocent about the degree to which reasoning can be and is conditioned by interests and all the factors he thought could be circumvented with assiduous enough application of analytic methodology. Descartes' problematic confidence in reason is a point we will need to pursue later, but at this juncture what you need to grasp is the picture of Descartes as a thinker excited about the potential of human reason as a newly acknowledged means of attaining cumulatively productive progress in inquiry and freeing us from authoritarianism and dogmatism.

7 Empiricism and Rationalism

As alluded to the aforementioned and as I will explain in the next chapter, Descartes' work was not revolutionary in the way it is usually thought to have been; nonetheless, it was pivotal for philosophy. The best evidence of this was its impact on British empiricism (see Glossary), particularly the work of John Locke (1632–1704) and David Hume (1711–1776). Contrary to Descartes' assumption that reason is itself a source of knowledge and not just of instrumental value, the empiricists, particularly Hume, argued that sensory experience is the sole source of knowledge and that reason is only the means of manipulating and employing the knowledge gained through sensory experience. The empiricists were themselves innovative thinkers but they addressed philosophical issues that essentially were defined by Descartes. Ironically, it was largely because of this that the empiricists failed to resolve the issues about knowledge that Descartes posed and to which they were responding – a failure most evident in Hume's skepticism or philosophical doubt that actual knowledge of the world is even possible.

As we proceed with discussion of Descartes, the contrast with Locke and Hume will often be in the background. The connections between Descartes, Locke, and Hume are difficult to sketch briefly, but they are highly significant, not just for understanding how philosophy developed after Descartes, but to better understand Descartes' own work by seeing the sorts of problems it raised for thinkers who followed and whose work was influenced by his.

What most needs to be noted regarding the empiricists in the present context is that Hume's skepticism was far more thoroughgoing than Descartes' own methodological doubt. It was so, less because Hume's analyses were more rigorous than because his presuppositions were more spare and tough-minded than Descartes' presuppositions. Hume made little effort to accommodate religious faith in his philosophizing, though he did sound properly pious when the occasion demanded it. More fundamental to the differences between them was that Hume was prepared to forgo Descartes' divinely guaranteed world of material things – to be discussed in Chapter 9 – as well as Locke's postulated but directly unknowable external reality of 'primary qualities' (See Glossary). Still more fundamental to their respective projects, Hume rejected *a priori* truth and knowledge. He equated *a priori* truth and knowledge, deriving from reason alone, with analytic or definitional truth and knowledge (See Glossary).

Contrary to British empiricism, which mainly revealed difficulties with Descartes' contentions, Continental rationalism (see Glossary) centered on endorsement of reliance on the *a priori* and was epitomized in the work of Benedict (Baruch) Spinoza (1632–77) and G. W. Leibniz (1646–1716). Leibniz and Spinoza also were innovative thinkers, but like the British empiricists, they mainly addressed issues about truth and knowledge that were given their structure and much of their substance by Descartes. However, the rationalism of Leibniz and Spinoza – the view that reason is not just instrumental but is itself a source of knowledge – was no more successful at resolving Descartes' problems than the empiricism of Locke and Hume, and eventually culminated, not in skepticism as it did in Britain, but in overly complex metaphysical systems that often became ends in themselves rather than credible explanatory systems (See Glossary). It is this metaphysical bent that makes the work of Descartes' rationalist successors of secondary importance for us, because it reveals less of the epistemological complications of Descartes' thought than the work of his empiricist successors. I hasten to reassure you, though, that our concern is Descartes' own work; the empiricists come into our discussion only occasionally.

8 Interim Summary

Lest you lose track of where we are, the core of the foregoing sections can be summed up in this way: gaining a solid grasp of Descartes' thought is essential to understanding modern and contemporary Anglo-European philosophy as well as one of the best ways of being introduced to philosophy. Descartes sought to establish what can be known with absolute certainty and to offer a method for acquiring absolute truth and so gaining indubitable knowledge. Rather than propound his views in lengthy treatises, he wrote a kind of 'how to' book: a surprisingly short series of six meditations that he invites readers to work through as if they were themselves thinking out the arguments. Descartes' goal was to enable discernment of what he thinks are intuitively clear ideas that once comprehended cannot be denied because of their evident truth.

Problems arise in several areas: there is no reflection on language's role in thought, too much is assumed about reason and truth, and too much is assumed about the nature of existent things, all of which indicate that Descartes' methodology was not applied as rigorously as he set out to apply it. Additionally, there are issues about the exact nature of Descartes' response to the intellectual turmoil of his time.

If Descartes' project had succeeded as he intended, he would have provided us with unquestionable knowledge about what we are, about God's existence, about why we sometimes go wrong, and about the material world. In addition, he would have provided us with a reliable procedure for discerning truth and acquiring knowledge – and he would have accomplished it all in one of the shortest philosophical texts ever written! Did Descartes' project succeed overall? The short answer is 'No,' but coming to understand the project and its successes and failures is a fascinating exercise in abstract thought and a beguiling invitation to do more.

9 Philosophy's Essential Characteristic

Philosophy as done in the Anglo-European tradition is a 2,500-year-old kind of questioning. Wilfrid Sellars perhaps best caught philosophy's essence, saying that '[t]he aim of philosophy is to understand how things in the broadest possible sense of the term hang together in the broadest possible sense of the term' (Sellars 1962, 37). Comprehensive understanding is what philosophy is all about, and the impetus to achieve comprehensive understanding is productive puzzlement about how things hang together, where 'things' can be concepts, ideas, or aspects and elements of the world. As Socrates so effectively demonstrated, the earmark of philosophical puzzlement is relentless questioning of what most never think to question.

Sometimes the questioning is driven purely by intellectual interest, sometimes it is driven by perplexity prompted by discoveries or oddities that challenge established ways of thinking and practices, often it is driven by glaring incompatibilities among beliefs different groups or individuals hold strongly. What matters is that questions are asked about basic ideas; that questions are asked about things that the great majority of people never give a thought and take completely for granted.

As we have seen, Descartes lived in a time when disturbing questions about how things hang together were being asked, a time when accepted beliefs about the world were beginning to be found insufficiently supported or at odds with new things being learned. Perhaps most notably, questions were being raised about geocentrism and heliocentrism, questions that had momentous implications for the orthodoxy of the day.

The debate prompted by Galileo ultimately was less about the status of the physical world than it was about the authority of the Church. There is nothing in Christian doctrine that specifically requires the Earth to be the center of the universe, but geocentrism is strongly implied by the story of Creation, which identifies creation of the physical universe with creation of our world. To maintain that our world is just one more planet among several circling the sun, therefore, was taken as denial of divine creation. It also was to dismiss as wrong or deluded authoritative figures like Ptolemy (100–170) and Tycho Brahe (1546–1601). The Church's defensive response to endorsement of heliocentrism was counterproductive in a way regrettably characteristic of institutional reactions to challenges. The response in effect sidelined the astronomical issue and made the debate one about dogmatism, over-rigid doctrines, and freedom of inquiry.

Descartes' reaction was complex. On the one hand, he cautiously decided not to publish a book he had been working on, titled *The World*, for fear he would end up before an ecclesiastical tribunal because he affirmed planetary motion in it. On the other hand, he tried to win favor with the faculty of theology by dedicating and introducing the *Meditations* as he did. More important, much of the aim of his efforts to develop a methodology for discerning absolute truth were, in effect, efforts to insure that challenges like Galileo's would never again arise and cause intellectual turmoil of the sort he saw around him. But regardless of our reservations about his ends, Descartes was certainly philosophizing; he was trying to understand how things in the broadest possible sense of the term hang together in the broadest possible sense of the term.

One of the features of philosophical questioning is that it extends to the very nature of the process of questioning itself. This is evident in how philosophy itself is currently being rethought by many. For some, philosophy continues to be the broadest and most abstract kind of inquiry we are capable of conducting, and one which may focus on anything at all that puzzles us. For others philosophy is a technical discipline concerned mainly with issues about the conceptual and the linguistic and far removed from the practical. For still others philosophy is applied, as in the case of medical and business ethics. More fundamentally, in our time traditional philosophy is challenged by historicist and postmodernist reconception of its most basic standard: truth. These are positions that allow no possibility of achieving answers to philosophical questions that do more than restate the perspectives and biases of historical periods.

However, adopting a historicist or postmodern position regarding truth is not abandonment of philosophy as Sellars characterizes it. One of the most influential postmodern challengers of traditional philosophy, Foucault, tells us that 'Western philosophy, since Descartes . . . has always been involved with the problem of knowledge.' Foucault adds that we could not count someone a philosopher who 'didn't ask . . . "What is knowledge?" or "What is truth?"' Despite his own relativistic position on truth and his criticism of traditional philosophy's conception of knowledge, Foucault insists that 'if my concern is with truth then I am . . . a philosopher' (Foucault 1980, 66).

We can take our cue from Foucault and say this much: whatever we may think about the nature of philosophy's proper subjects of study, whatever we may think about philosophy's proper methods, and whatever we may think about whether philosophy can yield ahistorical knowledge or only what is deemed right in a given time and from a given perspective, we are in agreement with both

Descartes and Foucault that questions about truth and knowledge are definitive of philosophy and philosophizing.

As we proceed, you must keep in mind that whatever you know or have been told about philosophy, in his *Meditations* Descartes raises questions about truth and knowledge, and in doing so he does philosophy in the truest sense. That his questions aim at discerning absolutes about the nature of the self and the existence of a God may now be unacceptable to many, but Descartes' little book is not only historically important, it is an archetype of the doing of philosophy.

10 Modern Philosophy and the Platonic Legacy

As should now be clear, our concern in this book is with Descartes' epistemology, his theory of knowledge. We will consider Descartes' metaphysical views, but his epistemology has priority if only because of the influence it had. Descartes' title, 'Father of Modern Philosophy,' does not attribute to Descartes only the initiation of a more up-to-date way of philosophizing than that of the Medievals and the Scholastics he followed. The term 'modern' in philosophy and intellectual history has a broader meaning referring to the priority of reason in all forms of inquiry, and to the common objective of acquiring knowledge to subjugate nature to human understanding and control.

Descartes initiated modern philosophy by shifting the focus of philosophical questioning from metaphysical speculation about ultimate reality and ethical inquiry heavily influenced by theology to investigation of how we know. This shift of focus gave methodological skepticism great importance and relocated the basis of certainty from authority and tradition to reason. Charles Sanders Peirce (1839–1914) summarized 'the spirit of Cartesianism' by saying that, for Descartes, 'philosophy must begin with universal doubt,' adding the point central to Cartesian thinking that 'the ultimate test of certainty is to be found in the individual consciousness' (Buchler 1955, 228). Certainty is to be found in consciousness in the sense that the ultimate test of what is the case is what is given to consciousness in an undoubtable way, in a way that reason will not allow to be doubted and requires to be accepted as true.

This grounding of certainty in consciousness is rejected by contemporary critics of modern philosophy. Hans-Georg Gadamer, a philosopher in the Continental tradition, rejects egocentric skepticism by rejecting the conviction that the ultimate test of certainty is to be found in individual consciousness. Gadamer argues that Nietzsche rightly demanded that we 'doubt more profoundly and fundamentally than ... Descartes [by] calling into doubt ... the testimony of human reflective consciousness' (Baynes 1987, 330). It is this more profound doubting that is missing in Descartes' failure to consider how language may condition thought and perception.

To give him his due, by trusting in the efficacy of analytic reasoning Descartes made a genuine advance on the Socratic and Platonic dialectic or discursive investigatory method of discerning truth. Descartes turned philosophical inquiry from a probing question-and-answer process into a breaking down into basic components of anything we believe or are inclined to believe and which is open to application of methodological skepticism. That he did so explains why his methodological proposals are easy to grasp in our time even by those most innocent of philosophy. Analysis is a methodology now deeply embedded in our still largely modern way of thinking. Most contemporaries are not inclined to question Cartesian reliance on analytic reasoning because it is fundamental to our way of thinking about knowledge and its acquisition. As anyone who espouses postmodern thinking will tell you – usually at length – most of us are still unreflectively committed to modernist thinking initiated in the seventeenth century. No wonder, then, that readers readily accept so much of what Descartes says in the *Meditations*.

More difficult to understand are some of Descartes' philosophical assumptions and maneuvers, a few of which are little more than leaps of faith despite his claims about thoroughgoing methodological doubt. However, to better appreciate these difficulties in Descartes' work, and to flesh out the context in which he wrote, we need to return briefly to Plato and Aristotle.

* * *

Parmenides initiated epistemology by arguing that real knowledge is only possible of what is eternal and unchanging. Anything less than knowledge of how things are eternally must remain mere 'opinion' because uncertain and vulnerable to amendment and revision. Very much in line with this idea, Plato thought mathematics to be the paradigm of knowledge, conceiving of mathematics as the objective study of real, eternal entities rather than as development of formal systems relating abstractions in defined ways. As for the world, the constantly changing world of 'appearances,' he believed we could only form opinions – temporary and changeable beliefs – about what is inherently unknowable because intrinsically unstable.

Aristotle was more practically inclined than his teacher, Plato, and cautioned against seeking more precision in inquiry than a subject allows. This caution was in part motivated by his appreciation of how strong is our inclination to learn about ourselves and our world. Aristotle held that we 'by nature . . . desire to know,' that because of our nature we want to learn as much as we can about everything that interests us (Kiernan 1962, 315). His view that some primordial human nature dictates our thirst for knowledge is now thought problematic; we have learned too much about human psychology to accept Aristotle's noble idea without reservations because we realize that too often what we seek is reassurance, even illusion, rather than knowledge. Certainly we need to modify his claim by considering how we sometimes do all we can precisely to avoid knowledge: to avoid unpleasant or disturbing facts, to maintain appearances, to steer clear of tough questions with even tougher answers.

What is of immediate interest in the present context is Aristotle's definition of truth, which was that a true proposition or statement is one which 'asserts that what is, is' (Kiernan 1962, 496). Achieving knowledge, then, is to be able to formulate statements which say how things are, and there is no explicit requirement that knowledge is limited to how things are eternally. But while unlike Plato, Aristotle tolerated varying degrees of knowledge, Descartes, who directly influenced modern epistemology more than Aristotle, followed Plato regarding knowledge. He shared with Plato the profound convictions that there is objective truth to be discerned, that we have ways of discerning it, and that once we do discern it, we have knowledge without qualification. There are no concessions made to the degree of precision a subject matter admits; the presupposition is that the subject matter of real knowledge is objective truth, and that objective truth always is determinate, exact, and absolute.

Many contemporaries, especially postmoderns, think that the notions of objective truth and certain knowledge are misconceived and do not think Plato's and Descartes' projects are possible or perhaps even coherent. Postmoderns believe that rather than Descartes having launched a worthwhile quest for truth and methodology for achieving it, what he actually did was initiate a fanciful and ultimately unproductive way of thinking about ourselves and our capacities that has persisted for centuries. What this shows is how philosophy in any given age is identified with how it is done in that age, and how different groups in a given age do philosophy differently. Postmoderns certainly do not philosophize as Descartes or Kant did, and many in the Cartesian tradition do not think postmoderns philosophize at all (O'Farrell 1989).

From an impartial point of view, it is clear that regardless of the extreme opposition between Cartesian and postmodern thinking, both sorts are encompassed by philosophy conceived in Sellars' way as inquiry at the broadest and most abstract level, but this is not always acknowledged. The modern certainty-oriented epistemological tradition encompassing Plato, Descartes, and Kant still defines philosophy for many contemporaries, and this tradition excludes postmodernist and other relativistic orientations to philosophy. For their part, the latter repudiate the modern tradition as profoundly misconceived, as based on what they judge to be wholly unworkable understandings of truth and knowledge. As a result, there is bitter opposition or dismissive indifference on both sides of the intellectual divide (Prado 2003).

The relevance of the contemporary split in philosophy to your introduction to Descartes is that it is inevitable that your reading of this book and of the *Meditations* will be influenced to some degree by how you have been influenced by the debate about philosophy in general and truth in particular. Nor is it necessary for you to have taken a course in philosophy or read philosophy for this influence to have occurred. The split in philosophy is reflected in all liberal arts and social science disciplines. There is not a sociologist, historian, political scientist, English professor, or cultural anthropologist who does not have a position on the objective or relative nature of truth.

11 Your Intellectual Milieu

Aside from how professional philosophers understand it, for most people the term 'philosophy' usually conjures up issues about ethics, freedom of the will, the soul, God, and perhaps 'ultimate reality.' Many turn to philosophy to resolve moral problems; to become clear about their freedom and responsibilities as agents; to understand their religious legacies or assumed obligations; to debate the existence of a God; and to wonder about the 'meaning' of existence. These projects usually begin with Cartesian assumptions, particularly that important truths are attainable by the use of reason and that conclusions reached through discursive reasoning will be correct independently of individual or group interests.

Today, many roughly describable as Nietzschean in their attitudes think that the Cartesian view of philosophy is little more than wishful thinking; that it basically is an exercise in communal rationalization of cherished beliefs and values. They think that the only truths we discover are the truths we make, that the methods and criteria we use are themselves products of our interpretive activities, and that our conceptions of reason and rationality themselves are historical and subject to change. For them, rather than philosophy being truth-attaining reasoning at its deepest and most rigorous, it is only how we work out our most basic commitments and how we justify our firmest beliefs. For them, rather than philosophy being thinking at its most general and abstract, it is how we construe thinking at its most general and abstract.

My point here is that your introduction to Descartes is taking place in an intellectual milieu that is, in its own way, as much in turmoil as was Descartes' intellectual milieu. There is, therefore, a real danger that you might see learning about Descartes as a purely historical exercise. This would be a mistake. Precisely because modern thinking is now challenged, it is crucial for you to understand it thoroughly. You need to understand it 'from the inside' in order to appreciate just what maintained and – to a point – still maintains it as intellectually dominant. Regardless of contemporary challenges, the Platonic/Cartesian construal of philosophy remains entrenched in Western culture; it is the construal that seems most natural and least problematic to many and the elements of which are most familiar. The person most innocent of philosophy readily recognizes the idea that truth is objective and the idea that knowledge is the discernment of such truth. The Nietzschean view, though increasingly widespread, especially in academia, still is relatively unfamiliar and somewhat elusive to many who fail to understand how there might not be eternal, capital-T Truth to discover and that there might be only historical small-t truths. These same many fail to understand how knowledge could be even partly a function of perspective, expectation, and decision.

Clearly, as you begin your study of Descartes, you will have modern or postmodern, Cartesian or Nietzschean sympathies and inclinations – whether or not you are aware of them as you begin. And just as clearly these inclinations and sympathies will affect how you read this book and the *Meditations*. This point should bring home to you how personal philosophizing is, and how reading Descartes may well raise pressing questions in your own mind about your own thought. From the outset you must be prepared, and in fact keen, to examine your own philosophical presuppositions and interpretive tendencies. The *Meditations* will provide you with the opportunity to do so, and you should appreciate that your introduction to Descartes will not be wholly successful unless you do as much wondering about your own thinking as you do about his.

* * *

It merits mention in the present context that some people turn to philosophy, not because they are moved by ethical or metaphysical questions, but because they are perplexed by knowledge itself. This is particularly likely to happen in times when there are significant intellectual changes taking place, as in Descartes' time and our own time. Despite the present dominance of the Platonic/Cartesian view of philosophy, anthropological, psychological, and sociological sophistication have made it seem, to many, that nothing can be true except from a particular perspective, at a particular time, and for a limited number of people or even a single individual.

Ample occasion has arisen to wonder about knowledge; about whether the traditional concept even makes sense. Still, most who do question the nature of knowledge find it difficult to accept the idea that what is known, the truth of something believed, is a function of temporal context and point of view. So, like Descartes, they try to establish that there is something which is always and forever true and that provides a base on which to ground everything else. For them the postmodern challenge to epistemology calls for more and better epistemology rather than reconception or abandonment of epistemology. Nonetheless, at least since the nineteenth century, some of those perplexed by knowledge have been convinced that there is something crucially wrong about both the felt-need for certainty and the belief that it is attainable.

The Cartesian way of philosophizing about truth and knowledge, traditional or modern epistemology, has as one of its basic presuppositions the idea that we can engage in intellectual investigation of knowledge itself in order to tell when we actually have knowledge. The anti-Cartesian or postmodern way of proceeding – trying to understand how what we know is a function of who we are and what we do – is, in effect, a matter of showing that traditional or modern epistemology simply cannot be done. It is to contend that knowledge is forever circumscribed by language and culture, by time and outlook, and so that no kind of inquiry, no matter how rigorous, can yield ahistoric certainty: knowledge independent of time, outlook, language, and culture. It is to contend that there is no neutral position from which we can investigate knowledge and judge it timelessly sound. It is to contend, therefore, that knowledge as Descartes conceived it is not only unattainable but is actually not a meaningful idea. It is, finally, to contend that epistemology must be naturalized, which is to say that epistemological questions must be shorn of their metaphysical trappings and turned over to empirical scientists to be considered and resolved in the context of empirical theories and data about thinking and learning.

What makes the timing of your introduction to Descartes, and thereby to modern philosophy, both opportune and risky is that postmodern challenges to modern philosophizing mean that you not only have to understand what Descartes was doing, you also have to assess the value and effectiveness of what he was doing. In philosophy, as in most intellectual endeavors, the availability of an alternative to something we have previously accepted unquestioningly poses an inescapable challenge. Whether you come to the *Meditations* with modern or postmodern sympathies, but especially with postmodern ones, properly understanding Descartes' little book requires you to seriously consider the opposed position. When you encounter a jarring difference of perspective, as you inevitably will in reading this text and the *Meditations*, you will appreciate the point of Nietzsche's remark: 'This is my way; where is yours? *The* way . . . does not exist' (Nietzsche 1968b, 307). But appreciating the point of Nietzsche's remark does not necessarily mean recognizing that he is right; you may well decide, again irrespective of your initial sympathies, that you agree with Descartes' fundamental presuppositions.

Unfortunately, the realization that there are alternatives to anything we believe firmly does not always occur, regardless of the diversity of thought and behavior encountered. It is perfectly possible to persist in never questioning what we believe and prize, regardless of how many opportunities to do so may occur. And if we do not, we are the losers for it. Learning about Descartes is your opportunity to think differently, something Foucault thought was an intellectual duty; it is your opportunity to fulfill 'the intellectual's reason for being,' which Foucault saw as '[m]odifying one's own thought' (Foucault 1986, 9; 1989, 303).

12 Getting the Most from this Book

This book's preparation was guided by the idea that an introduction to a particular philosopher should not try to be comprehensive because trying to cover everything inevitably results in a leveling of the important, the less important, and what is only of marginal importance. A better and more effective way to provide an introduction to a philosopher, especially a philosopher as influential as Descartes, is to engage with the most central ideas and arguments that define the particular philosopher's thought and work. Descartes' writings lend themselves to this approach; in particular, the *Meditations* are self-contained and present precisely what is most central in Descartes' contribution to philosophy. The *Meditations* also are Descartes' most engaging work because they are written in such a way that readers can work their way through the six meditations as if they themselves were writing them. Descartes' 'I' is intended to be the reader's 'I.' In fact, the second meditation cannot achieve what it is supposed to achieve if readers do not think it out as if they themselves were originating the argument.

To proceed, you have three options open to you regarding this book and the *Meditations*. You can read this book first and then the *Meditations*; you can read this book and the *Meditations* together, alternatively reading a chapter here and the relevant meditation or vice versa; or you can read the *Meditations* first and then this book. If you are reading this book as a main or supplementary text in a philosophy course, your instructor will have something to say about which of these options is most appropriate, but in my view, the most productive way to proceed is a combination of the aforementioned options. I strongly recommend that you read the *Meditations* and this book together in the following way:

Read this Introduction (Chapter 1) first, and then read Chapter 2. Next, read Descartes' preliminary material in the *Meditations*: the letter to the Sorbonne, the short preface to the reader, and the synopsis of the meditations. Then read Chapter 3 in this book, on the first meditation. When you have finished Chapter 3, read Descartes' first meditation. Once you get through the first three chapters in this book, Descartes' preliminary material, and the first meditation, reverse the process with meditations two through six; that is, read each of the remaining five meditations first, and then read each of the appropriate chapters in this book – Chapters 4 through 9. Read the Conclusion to this book, Chapter 10, only when you have finished the other chapters and all six meditations.

I realize this sounds overly complicated, but I know from long experience teaching Descartes that it is the most productive way for novices to proceed through the material. Proceeding in the suggested manner will insure that you do not miss important subtleties and problems in each meditation, but it will especially insure that your progress in understanding Descartes is productively cumulative and, most important, that you engage personally with his thought.

13 Reading Philosophy

At this point it is a good idea to caution you against initial frustration. Some of what you read as you begin this book and the *Meditations* will not be clear until you read a fair bit more of each. This is to be expected because it is in the very nature of reading philosophy that much of what you read in the *Meditations* requires you to rethink ideas you hold as well as ideas you do not know you hold and emerge only when you encounter new ideas that challenge them. Reading philosophy also requires that you grasp new ideas unrelated to any you already hold. The former requirement makes reading philosophy challenging or provocative, fascinating or exasperating; the latter requirement makes reading philosophy demanding. But both requirements prompt an important piece of advice that, unfortunately, few readers take seriously. The advice is easy to give but difficult to follow: reread everything.

Understanding a philosophical text requires several readings. If you want to prove this to yourself, go back and reread a page or two of Sections 1 through 10, earlier, and underline what you think are the most important things said. Put the book aside for a few hours or a day, then reread the same pages. You will be surprised to find that you will want to underline different parts. What you should understand from this little exercise is that grasping philosophical ideas is a dynamic and ongoing process. Every line you read affects and conditions your understanding both of lines you have already read and of those you have still to read, and every hour that an idea is at the back of your mind allows for subtle alterations to that idea.

I advise that you read a work in philosophy at least three times. First, a philosophical work should be read once through without too much concern with what may be initially obscure or complex. The point is to get a rough idea of the sort of work it is, of what it emphasizes, and what claims are made and conclusions drawn. Second, the work should be reread, but much more thoughtfully and carefully. After the second reading, you should set the work aside for a day or two and think about some of the things that most struck you about it. You will find it surprising how on your second time through the work, not only will difficult passages be clearer, you will see connections between parts that you missed on the first reading. You will find it even more surprising how rereading presents you with a slightly different totality; you will find that different parts of the work emerge as more prominent than they did at first.

The third reading is different, and it is when you really begin to engage with a philosophical work. On reading a work for the third time, read it in what is best described as a wary way. That is, you should be looking for things that strike you as strained or anomalous; you should also be looking for things that seem at odds with other parts of the work. You should be especially sensitive to ideas that emerge but are not argued for or made explicit in the text. You also need to be sensitive to complex discussions that leave you perplexed or appear to come to too little. On the third reading the work must be read probingly; you should look beneath the surface by asking such questions as: What does someone have to believe or be thinking to say this? Why should someone think this to be obvious, to not need argument or support? It is also important to be alert to ordinary words being used in special ways. The author may be trying to win acceptance of something by trading on the ordinary sense of a word while using it in a special way.

* * *

The importance of the foregoing point about philosophers' use of ordinary terms in special ways merits fuller discussion because it so often is what trips up novices and why rereading is so important to understanding. The most relevant example in the present context – and there are many more – is when Descartes talks about ideas or the having of ideas. I explore this point in Chapter 4, but briefly put, it is in talking about awareness as the having of ideas that Descartes effectively assimilates sensation to reflection, feeling to thought. This is seldom obvious to novices, but it is of crucial importance. What Descartes does is that by using 'idea' and 'ideas' to refer to all the contents of consciousness, he turns the having of sensations into the entertaining of ideas in the mind – ideas the causes of which are believed to be events in the body. Descartes takes himself to be talking about what is perfectly familiar to us, but what he is really doing is purveying a particular conception of the nature of awareness or consciousness.

Descartes' conception is of consciousness as the having of 'internal' representations – that is, internal to the mind in a way that makes events in the body 'external' to the mind. Notice that this conception does not allow us to distinguish between being sentient and being conscious. In fact, Descartes did not think non-conscious entities, animals of all sorts, were actually sentient; he thought non-conscious entities were robot-like and had no feeling. Thanks to Descartes, it actually became fashionable in some circles to think that animals could not feel pain and to be indifferent to their supposedly only apparent suffering.

I explore Descartes' conception of consciousness hereafter, but at this juncture the point I want to make is that too many readers accept his conception by default simply by not recognizing that Descartes' use of the term 'idea' entails a conception of consciousness. By talking easily about the contents of awareness as the having of ideas, Descartes too often succeeds in winning acceptance of the notion that our awareness of the world is purely a matter of having mental copies in our minds of the things that make up what then becomes an external world – an external world that includes our own bodies and that suddenly becomes unknowable in a direct manner and so epistemically problematic.

In treating consciousness as the having of ideas, therefore, Descartes surreptitiously but effectively reconceives the nature of awareness by his special use of terms and succeeds in isolating us from the world as subjects the contents of whose consciousness are a series of internal events: presentations in the mind of things outside the mind – with some of what is outside the mind being events in the body, such as sensations and pains. And because Descartes defines ideas as comprising all that we are aware of, the problem arises as to how we ever manage to gain knowledge about what is outside our minds – but more on all of this later. The point here is to illustrate how an apparently innocuous use of language, a particular use of the term 'idea,' establishes a philosophical position that likely will not be recognized as being a position by many readers and be taken as articulation of the common view. Reading philosophy is difficult, and it must be read repeatedly, carefully, thoroughly, and warily to gain full understanding of what is going on.

14 Problems in Reading

Unfortunately, many people new to philosophy think that reading it is a matter of learning about philosophy, as is the case with subjects like history or geology. You should read philosophy to learn to do it, not just to learn about it. 'Philosophy' is less the name of a discipline or cohesive body of knowledge than of a way of thinking. This is what makes being introduced to philosophy particularly difficult, because learning philosophy requires learning actually to do philosophy, not just assimilating information about philosophy.

There are a number of other problems that plague the reading of philosophy by those new to it. Authors' repeated use of particular terms often goes unnoticed; you must be alert for inconsistencies and ambiguities in the use of key terms, and aware that the more often terms are used, the likelier it is that ambiguities or inconsistencies will creep into their use. Philosophers often make certain favored terms do too much work; Descartes' use of 'idea' is a prime example, as you will see.

You also must be alert to lack of contrast: when something is claimed in a work, you have to consider whether there is a significant alternative. Some philosophical claims are so general or hedged about with qualifications that they are actually compatible with just about anything. You need to think of possible counterexamples to claims made, of what would conflict with whatever is being claimed. If nothing would conflict, then nothing significant is being claimed.

Again, you need to keep in mind criteria for correctness. When claims are made, ask yourself how you would go about deciding if the claims are warranted or not and how they might be established as true. In most of what we encounter outside philosophy this question is usually answerable in empirical terms: that is, we can check to see if some claimed state of affairs is or is not the case. But when something is problematic in philosophy, we cannot just go and look; we cannot settle issues by observation or experimentation with overtly accessible things, events, or situations. This is why it is necessary to be clear on what arguments supporting a philosophical claim say regarding what counts as the claim being correct.

One favored way philosophers have of supporting their claims, and which often poses difficulties for novices, is 'thought experiments' or carefully described imagined situations to support or impugn a claim. The object of such experiments is to illustrate the acceptability or unacceptability of a contention. In a thought experiment a situation is depicted in which what is at issue is described as routine to see if it is credible or not in terms of our preparedness to take the imagined situation as a matter of course or to reject it as unbelievable or confused. The underlying assumption is that so long as we are careful to be objective, our intuitions will afford reliable guidelines, since they are taken to be rooted in our rationality. However, in using devices like thought experiments, we may only be favoring intuitions that are themselves problematic and only products of our training and expectations, rather than being fully rational.

The penultimate problem I will mention here again has to do with problematic terms, but this time with readers' grasp, rather than authors' use of them. It is crucial that you use a good dictionary. The short Glossary I provide should be of help to you, but it cannot begin to replace a good dictionary. Moreover, given the esoteric nature of philosophical writing, a 'good' dictionary is not a handy abridged edition. You need an unabridged edition, and once you have it, you need to use it. If you experience any hesitation at all when you encounter an unfamiliar term, look it up. I cannot stress this too much. Over the years, time and time again I have had to deal with confusion and unproductive misinterpretation that were due to simple errors about terms used in texts and lectures.

Lastly, you should note that something people too often forget or perversely ignore when they read philosophy is common sense. Because philosophy is thought to be profound and difficult, people often read it in an overly credulous way, assuming that what they are reading is too deep to be immediately clear. In fact, one sometimes feels that when people read philosophy they expect and even want obscurity. But philosophers are as capable of being wrong or unclear as anyone else, and depth should not be assumed on the basis of difficulty. You must not be afraid to consider that something you encounter in reading philosophy is confused or wrongheaded. You should not think, as many do, that if you do not understand a text, it must be very deep and complex; it might just be badly written or muddled.

The other side of this is that you should not automatically resist what is initially obscure or strange. A philosophical work must be read in as open-minded and flexible a way as possible. Philosophers are concerned to change their readers' thinking at the most funda-mental level, and if you are to benefit from what they say, you need to allow your deepest assumptions and values to be challenged. A difficult balance must be struck between being gullible and being open-minded. Consider a claim you will encounter in what follows: Descartes will contend that at this precise moment you may be dreaming. You may feel inclined to dismiss this as absurd, but you must seriously consider the claim as a worthwhile novel perspective, even if adopted only for the sake of argument. At the same time, you must keep Descartes' claim in perspective as a device intended to facilitate methodological doubt and not make more of it than you should.

15 Some Practical Considerations

There are several translations and editions of the *Meditations* avail-able. One of the better ones is a translation by John Cottingham, which has a useful introduction by Bernard Williams and selections from Descartes' replies to objections made to his *Meditations* (Cottingham 1995).

In Cottingham's translation, the *Meditations* run from page 12 through page 62 – that is just 51 pages. Most philosophy books are more like three-hundred pages and often considerably longer. I mention the length of the *Meditations* to put the advice about rereading in perspective. If you take the advice – and I strongly recommend you do – the *Meditations* in effect work out to be a 153-page work, still only about half the length of the average philosophy book.

* * *

If you are new to philosophy, as this book assumes you are, the foregoing may seem initially overwhelming, but I can promise that after sufficient reading not only will it be easier, you will be intrigued. Think of the chapters that follow as an adventure in intellectual self-development, as well as an introduction to Descartes, and think of this chapter as equipping you for that adventure. Recalling my advice about rereading, at this point you need to recheck your equipment.

CHAPTER 2

DESCARTES AND HIS PROJECT

René Descartes is usually pictured in histories of philosophy and in books more focused on his work as an intellectual revolutionary. He is cast as someone concerned about introducing something novel to philosophical thinking, as Galileo introduced something novel to astronomical thinking. This portrayal of Descartes is due in part to his innovations in mathematics (Matson 2000, 317) and partly to too-ready association of him with innovators like Galileo. This association casts Descartes, by implication, as an enthusiastic disparager of medieval methods and assumptions (Debus 1978). And, it is true that the Church's reaction to his philosophical writings tends to support the association. However, this common view of Descartes and his philosophical project as revolutionary is dubious because it at least seriously misconstrues his motivation.

Rather than to revolutionize philosophy, what Descartes actually tried to achieve with his admittedly innovative skeptical method was really a very conservative objective. He tried to ensure that human knowledge would never again be as radically challenged and disrupted as it was by his contemporary, Galileo, and others. Descartes saw challenges to established views, and the ensuing disruptions, as only possible because of prior error. His project, therefore, was all about trying to preclude further disruptive intellectual challenges by expunging error: he tried to ground knowledge in utterly reliable, unchanging truths. He believed that once we discerned eternal truths, we could go about the detailed business of developing knowledge with the assurance that our cognitive achievements would never again prompt the sort of upheaval Galileo caused and that they would stand for all time.

The crucial thing to understand about Descartes' objective, and how he could have it as an objective, is that he thought knowledge to be of a piece, to be ultimately unitary in a way we now have difficulty understanding. For Descartes, knowledge was not to be carved up into various disciplines; it was not to be divided into the physical sciences, the social sciences, and the arts. And because he deemed knowledge to be unitary, Descartes thought it was capable of being grounded on a small number of fundamental truths.

As C. P. Snow (1905–80) once remarked, our culture distinguishes sharply between the humanities on the one hand and the sciences on the other. Additionally, it thinks of the sciences and humanities as themselves divided into areas and sub-areas, such as biology and chemistry, literature and history. This fragmentation of knowledge precludes the possibility that diverse disciplines and forms of inquiry could have the same grounds and be capable of justification in the same way. Descartes thought knowledge was whole, of a piece, and totally rational, so that it was possible to ground it all on a relatively few truths, and that once we had those basics, and given enough time and effort, we could develop all of the rest of possible knowledge. More strikingly still, Descartes genuinely thought that he could articulate for us all we needed to begin the ages-long task of discerning and formulating all that can be known. That was his enterprise: no less than to provide the means for the achievement of all possible knowledge. There then would be no need, no occasion for further intellectual revolutions and the chaos they entail.

* * *

The initial and most important item Descartes sought in his enterprise was a single unquestionable truth to serve as the base for an inverted pyramid of ever more complex truths and knowledge. This first truth would provide a fundamental and absolutely reliable standard, enabling us to test by comparison with it anything else which we might think to be true. Descartes reminds us that Archimedes needed 'nothing more than a fixed and immovable fulcrum,' and Descartes believed he would have his own epistemic fulcrum if he could 'find a single truth which is certain and indubitable' (Descartes 2, 23 [1, 149]. Note that primary references to Descartes' *Meditations*, like the one just made, will refer to Descartes, rather than the editor of the main edition used, and will include the number of the meditation to facilitate the use of other editions and comparisons of editions. The accompanying page numbers in the primary references are those of Laurence Lafleur's 1951 edition of the *Meditations*, which is the least expensive and perhaps the most widely used, witness that the 1989 reprint I happen to have is no less than the thirty-first reprinting. To further facilitate comparison of editions and translations, primary references also include the same reference, in square brackets, to the 1969 standard edition of Descartes' collected works edited by Elizabeth Haldane and G. R. T. Ross. I also cite Haldane and Ross separately. Occasionally, where I think the translation better in one or another respect, I refer to the 1995 reprint of Cottingham's 1986 edition of the *Meditations*. These secondary references give Cottingham's name, as editor, and the date and page number, as is standard. See Selected Bibliography for publishers' details regarding all citations. Note also that because footnotes and endnotes often are ill-advisedly ignored, all my notes and references are given parenthetically in the text.)

Descartes thought that to get the necessary utterly reliable sample of truth he sought, he needed to subject everything he believed to the most stringent doubt in order to find at least one thing that he could not doubt and that would therefore be revealed as absolutely true. He proceeded to withhold belief from anything 'not entirely certain and indubitable' just as he would from what appeared to him to be clearly false (Descartes 1, 17 [1, 145]). A different translation of this passage, which is clearer, has Descartes being 'no less careful to withhold . . . assent from matters which are not entirely certain and indubitable than from those which appear . . . false' (Haldane and Ross 1969, Vol. I, 145). However translated, the point is that Descartes' methodology was to dismiss as false anything which was open to the slightest doubt. This is not to say that he judged anything uncertain to be actually false, as that would be as questionable as judging it true, but rather that he set out to treat as false anything not indubitably true. His main operating principle was that discovery of truth could only be as certain as the thoroughness of his methodological skepticism.

* * *

What Descartes is doing in applying methodological doubt is proceeding on the assumption that if we set aside everything in our minds that is even slightly uncertain, we will be left only with absolute knowledge – assuming anything at all remains. Descartes, of course, seems never to have gone so far as doubting that anything would survive methodological doubt. This is one of the ways that his general philosophical approach is undermined. The point is that it is difficult to imagine how Descartes could have thought up and then applied his methodological doubt if not already sure that it would reveal one or more absolute truths. As a postmodern might argue, the very conception of methodological doubt, as Descartes presents it, entails that there is at least one indubitable truth to be discerned, which is Descartes' objective and should not be his – tacit – starting point.

If just what Descartes is thinking seems hard to understand, it helps to appreciate that he thought of truth as a simple and evident property: a property discernible by the 'natural light' of reason, just as a color is discernible by ordinary light. Descartes believed that once we clear them of obfuscating false beliefs, our minds perceive truth in almost literally the same way that our eyes perceive color. The importance of this visual metaphor, and it is actually a stretch to call it a metaphor as Descartes employed it, is difficult to overestimate because, for Descartes, recognition or realization of truth was a form of perception conceived on the model of sight. In fact, at times it seems that it is the other way around and that seeing is metaphorical and perception of truth literal: do not forget that visual perception is a bodily sense, while perception of truth is an integral element of being a mind. (Note that while I have spoken and will continue to speak of 'awareness' in general, in what follows 'perception' mostly is used to designate specific forms of sensory awareness, such as vision.)

Supposedly, once we perceive and recognize a single undoubtable truth, we have a paradigm, a standard, by which to judge all other apparent or possible truths. We then can test potential truths, the thinking goes, by comparing them with our indubitable sample. The parallel is to comparing colored objects, such as fabric swatches, to a preferred sample. The similarity or lack of similarity between two swatches compared is obvious to us on looking at them, at least in unproblematic cases. Descartes thought that having a single indubitable truth is having a wholly unproblematic sample of truth to which we can then compare other beliefs, just as we compare fabric swatches to test similarity of color. He thought there would be an obvious similarity between true beliefs: a similarity actually more obvious to reason than the color similarity is to visual perception. He further thought that the lack of similarity between true and false beliefs would be equally obvious. So as long as we are able to discern just one unquestionable, undoubtable truth, we can compare any other belief or claim to it and so judge if that claim or belief is true or false. We will know the claim or belief we are testing to be true, as our sample is true, if it has the same 'clarity and distinctness' as our sample truth. And we will know the belief or claim we are testing to be false, or at least questionable, if it falls short of our standard to any degree.

Regardless of how sophisticated Descartes' thinking was in most respects, there is something almost touchingly naïve about the idea that once we have a sample of truth in hand, we can test other beliefs or potential beliefs by simple comparison. Notice that there is no hint here of the complexities introduced by interpretation, by point of view. This is where the vision metaphor shows itself to be so pivotal and, at the same time, so restrictive of Descartes' thinking. He believed – as in fact many people do – that we can settle disputes about what is or is not true by just looking. He gives no thought at all to how what we see is so often a function of what we want or expect to see, nor does he consider how seldom we encounter ideas, things, or events that present themselves completely unambiguously.

It is important to dwell a moment on Descartes' visual metaphor to better understand the sort of thing you should be alert to in reading philosophy. The analogy between comparing true beliefs and similarly colored fabric swatches should remind us that often, if the colors are very close, we cannot readily tell if two swatches actually are the same color. The point is that in comparisons, when there is ambiguity or varying perspectives, as there usually are, we have to make decisions; we need to make up our minds about whatever is at issue because what we see simply is not enough to resolve the question. Descartes does not allow for inconclusive comparisons because he relies heavily – we might say too heavily – on 'clarity and distinctness' to resolve any ambiguity or uncertainty that might complicate comparisons. The clarity and distinctness of an idea – of our sample of truth – is supposed to take care of doubt. For Descartes' clarity and distinctness perceived by the 'natural light of reason' is always decisive – recall Peirce's remark, earlier (Buchler 1955, 228).

Consider that even if we granted Descartes' point about the sample of truth and clear and distinct similarity, we would still have to wonder just how many truths there are that both have the required degrees of clarity and distinctness and are of practical interest to us. It is easy enough to find credible examples of what Descartes is calling clear and distinct truths in basic arithmetic, but what about in history, psychology, or interpersonal relations?

There are other questions that arise when it becomes evident that Descartes is stipulating and assuming quite a lot about intellectual perception and comparison of beliefs: If true beliefs are similar in virtue of recognizable clarity and distinctness shared with obvious truth, what about false beliefs? Are false beliefs simply different from true beliefs, but diversely so? Or are false beliefs all characterized by a similarity either not mentioned or not thought of by Descartes?

A trickier point is that if successful comparison of beliefs with the sample of truth is thought by Descartes as confirming the putative truth of the compared beliefs, a question arises about the confirmed or newly established truths: are they true because the comparison establishes that the particular compared beliefs are true in terms of their content? This seems unlikely, as it is difficult to see how comparison with a known truth establishes the truth of the content of different beliefs. It seems, then, that what is established in the comparison is the truth itself of the compared beliefs; it seems that their truth itself is apprehended in the comparison, in virtue of the similitude of our conscious experience of the compared beliefs and of our standard of truth. In other words, from the way Descartes puts things, it seems that what is perceived with clarity and distinctness by the natural light of reason is truth *per se*, not, as we might put it, particular true contents of compared beliefs.

If you reflect for a moment you should see that there is an important difference between, on the one hand, grasping that proposition A is true, grasping that proposition B is true, and that proposition C is true, because what A, B, and C, respectively, state is the case, and, on the other hand, grasping something about all three propositions that makes all three true. You might think, initially, that of course the content of each proposition is what is seen to be true, but that is not as clear as it might be in the *Meditations*. It most often seems that truth is an additional property of beliefs and propositions or statements and that, as such, it is this additional property that we apprehend clearly and distinctly by the natural light of reason, quite aside from the content of the propositions and beliefs.

*   *   *

The key part of the Cartesian methodology for discerning truth and developing knowledge is application of analysis. This is the process of breaking down complex beliefs and potential beliefs into their simplest components and testing the truth of each of those components by comparison with touchstone evident truths. If each of the various components of a complex belief or potential belief individually passes the comparative test for truth, if each component matches the standard of truth in clarity and distinctness, then the truth of the complex belief or potential belief is established by simple addition of the tested components. This is the essence of the Cartesian method: to analyze the complex into its most basic components, and to test those basic components by comparing them to an indubitable sample of truth. Only when the various components have been found to be individually true can the aggregate be accepted as true.

Additionally, what is gained through the analytic/comparative process is not just the establishment of a complex belief or potential belief as true, because once established as true, a complex belief itself serves as a known, reliable component of even more complex beliefs. This is how Descartes thought we would eventually build up knowledge as a complete ideational mirror-image of reality, how we would learn all there is to know. Of course, human knowledge will always be restricted by the limited nature of our intellects. Some metaphysical truths, such as the exact nature of God, for instance, must always elude us, but they are not necessary for us to know.

As you, no doubt, expected by now, questions again arise. At this point, the most pressing question is this: What makes Descartes think that all complex beliefs are analyzable into distinct components that can be individually tested for truth? And what makes him think that beliefs established as true are additive in the sense that we can string them together to constitute more complex beliefs? It may be credible enough with respect to physics or chemistry to claim that complex beliefs can be broken down into their constitutive components, but what about sociology or history? Even in a problematically scientific discipline like economics, what are the simple components of a belief as basic as that individuals aim to maximize their net-worth? Once we look at it closely, this belief quickly reveals that at least some of its elements are psychological, not economic. The idea of maximizing net-worth is not intelligible if we do not factor in the desire to have a greater net-worth and the intention to increase net-worth, and desires and intentions do not lend themselves to Descartes' form of analysis and comparison.

* * *

Aside from grounding human knowledge on indubitable truth, Descartes had a number of secondary objectives. Uppermost among these was to understand the nature of what he called our 'ideas' as well as the origins of our ideas. By an 'idea' Descartes meant anything present to the mind, anything that is an object of awareness. For Descartes, thought or thinking just is having ideas: '*Thought* . . . covers . . . everything that exists in us in such a way that we are immediately conscious of it'; Descartes adds that '[i]*dea* is a word by which I understand the form of any thought'

(Descartes, *Arguments*, Haldane and Ross 1969, Vol. II, 52.). What this means, and what many readers of the *Meditations* miss, is that as was mentioned in Chapter 1, it follows from Descartes' conception and definition of thought that sensing something, as in experiencing cold or pain or the taste of strawberries, is having ideas and therefore having thoughts. In short being aware, being conscious, is, for Descartes, having or 'entertaining' ideas. To be a thinking being is to have ideas, and to be a sentient being is to have ideas. We are minds and bodies only in an extended sense; basically what we are is minds, and to be a mind, to be a thinking thing, is to have ideas. When we sense something in or around our bodies, we have ideas. Whatever is going on in our bodies and around them is conveyed and presented to us as ideas.

Descartes' conception of ideas was new and had significant ramifications for philosophy, especially beginning with the empiricism of Locke and Hume. As Richard Rorty (1931–2007) puts it, 'the modern use of the word *idea* derives . . . from Descartes. The novelty was the notion of a single inner space in which bodily and perceptual sensations, mathematical truths, moral rules, the idea of God, moods of depression, and all the rest . . . were objects of quasi-observation' (Rorty 1979, 48–50).

Closely related to his conception of awareness as the having of ideas, is Descartes' conception of the mind as transparent to itself. Descartes explicitly disallows that there might be something in the mind – which can only be an idea in his sense – of which we might not be conscious. He insists that 'nothing can exist in the mind . . . of which [the mind] is not conscious' (Descartes, *Reply to Objections IV*, Haldane and Ross 1969, Vol. II, 115). Also, in a 1641 letter to the Reverend Mersenne, Descartes says: 'by the term "idea" I mean in general everything which is in our mind when we conceive of something, no matter how we conceive it' (Kenny 1970, 105). A theoretical postulation like Freudian unconscious desires would have been laughable, if not incoherent, for Descartes. If something is in the mind, it is an idea present to us.

Ideas, then, are the contents of consciousness, and ideas are, by nature and by definition, present to the mind. But their very presence, their existence as the contents of awareness, raises the question of where ideas come from, of what causes minds to have ideas. Like everything else, with the single exception of God, ideas must have causes; they must arise from something. Descartes' next move is to consider the causes of ideas, and he does so in order to establish which ideas represent real things and which ideas arise for other reasons, such as error or illusion.

For Descartes, all ideas are potentially representations of real things, but some in fact are not. Part of his methodology is to first attend to ideas neutrally, to entertain them while reserving judgment about whether or not they do represent something real. The exception is, again, God. As we will see in Chapters 5 and 8, one of Descartes' basic claims is that to entertain the idea of God is to understand that God exists. He offers two arguments, one his own, one a traditional argument, to demonstrate not only that the idea of God represents a reality, but that it must do so.

Thinking of all the contents of awareness as initially 'neutral' ideas entertained in the intellect but not assented to, enabled Descartes to be skeptical about the possible causes of ideas without too readily impugning some ideas and too hastily inclining to accept others as veridical. For example, we are naturally more dubious about something seen dimly through a fog than about the feel of something heavy in our hand, but for Descartes, since ideas in themselves are simply the contents of the mind, they cannot be taken as more or less veridical just by how they present themselves to the mind. Once more, the all-important exception is the idea of God.

Descartes' idea of an idea is often interpreted as what we think of as a mental image. This interpretation is difficult to avoid, but it does not do justice to what Descartes means; it is too simplistic an understanding of the visual metaphor so ingrained in his thinking. As will become clear in the next chapter, understanding oneself as a thinking thing cannot be effectively done if doing so is only thinking of oneself as having mental images or pictures in the head.

The trouble is that when we try to offer a more adequate account of what it is to have an idea before the mind, Descartes' idea of an idea begins to grow elusive. I will not pursue this point here, though I will return to it; I mention the point only so you will keep in mind that it will not do to understand the entertaining of Cartesian ideas merely as having mental images. At this point it suffices to say that Descartes' view of awareness as the entertaining of ideas is conception of awareness as the having of something present to the mind, on the model of seeing something, where what is present to the mind may or may not be a representation of something in the sense that what is present to the mind is the effect of some reality external to the mind. Putting things this way allows us to avoid the issue of just what ideas are for the moment.

What is most important to note regarding the having of ideas is that even having ideas which are taken as awareness of one's own body is the having of ideas present to the mind, the causes of which need to be established. Regardless of the immediacy of their apparent causes, ideas we have of the most intense and vivid sensory experiences might not be veridical. Establishing what ideas are ideas of, must always be indirect. First, ideas are had; they present themselves to the mind. Only secondly may there be acceptance of or 'assent to' the ideas as genuine perceptions of something: even if that something is an event in the body, such as pain or hunger or some other bodily sensation. For Descartes, the body is no more reliable a cause of ideas than is anything else – always excepting God.

* * *

On first reading, Descartes' conception of awareness may seem plausible because we understand how awareness even of goings-on in our own bodies is the result of a complicated neurophysiological process involving stimulated nerves and culminating in various sorts of brain activity. But Descartes' view is quite different from this scientific one that we take for granted. For him, even the events in the higher parts of the brain, events which we conceive of as actually the instantiation of awareness, were only further causes of ideas occurring in a still different realm: the autonomous, non-material, conscious mind.

What must be appreciated about Descartes' picture of awareness as the having of ideas is that aside from the issues it raises, the assimilation of every kind of awareness to the having of ideas is essential to Descartes' project because it enables his holistic skepticism, his methodology of universal doubt designed to discern absolute truth. The assimilation enables both conception and application of the methodology by letting him question the veracity of all instances of awareness without regard to their degree of immediacy or anything else. By conceiving of awareness as the having of ideas, and of ideas as purely mental occurrences located in the nonmaterial mind, Descartes effectively detaches instances of awareness that are perceptions, as opposed to thoughts about mathematics, say, from their causes – including sensations or internal bodily perceptions. This means that, on his scheme, no one idea is any different in epistemic status from any other; no instance or sort of awareness has greater or lesser immediate veracity in the order of knowledge regardless of how it is experienced – with the notable exception of the idea of God.

All ideas are, in themselves, neutral presentations to the mind, and as we will see in the next chapter, the mind is wholly independent of everything in its ideational content – independent of everything but God. Whether some ideas are veridical representations of something other than themselves always is a further question. For instance, our tendency to trust touch more than sight is pointless on Descartes' scheme; instances of touch and sight are both equally neutral ideas presented to the mind. Until one or another is judged to relate to something real, the ideas are simply the constituents of a thinking mind. As will emerge in Chapter 7, the initial representational neutrality of ideas also is crucial to Descartes' attempt to account for error in the fourth meditation.

The assimilation of all the contents of awareness to ideas is perhaps one of the most difficult notions to grasp in understanding Descartes. But the difficulty is not just a matter of the novelty of his conception of the mind and its contents. A good part of the difficulty is that many new to Descartes accept the conception without reflection on what it means. That is, many people reading Descartes for the first time tend to understand his account of the mind and of ideas in terms of their own comprehension of awareness as the having of thoughts and sensations. They see Descartes' talk of ideas and the mind as only the use of archaic terms for consciousness as presently understood in terms of stimuli and brain events. This anachronistic interpretation is wrong-headed. Most simply put, contemporary understanding of consciousness sees it as a series of effects of neural stimulation and activity. On this understanding, the mind or consciousness is itself a complex effect, the consequence of ongoing neural activity. But for Descartes the mind precedes its contents; it is an independent substance that comes to have ideas. Most of this will become clearer hereafter, but the point here is that Descartes' conception of the mind and its contents is very different from our present one. As you read this book and the *Meditations*, you cannot afford to overlook the specialness of the Cartesian conception of the mind; you cannot afford to be lulled into thinking that a quite alien conception differs from your own only in being couched in outdated language.

For Descartes, then, being a conscious entity is first and foremost to be a pure consciousness entertaining ideas. Given this, it must be appreciated fully that awareness of one's own body, as in the case of having a headache or just flexing one's fingers, is having ideas that are just as problematic as ideas about the world external to the mind. In other words, all ideas stand in need of being grounded or proven to be true; all need to be shown worthy of belief.

* * *

If the heart of Cartesian epistemology is methodological doubt, the most important metaphysical implication of Descartes' conception of the mind and its contents is that we are, each of us, pure consciousnesses that achieve knowledge of ourselves and the world by having ideas and establishing that some of those ideas represent – were caused by – realities independent of the ideas they cause in our minds. As Cartesian minds, we are not spatial; consciousness is not the sort of thing that takes up room. Other people, material objects, and even our own bodies are, in the first instance, ideas we entertain and which must be shown to truly represent objective realities before they can be taken as actual perceptions and as yielding knowledge. For us to legitimately accept that we do have a body, that there are other people and material objects, the Cartesian epistemological project must succeed: we must be able to discriminate among ideas that are truly representational and ideas that are not. Otherwise all of alleged human knowledge remains so much unsubstantiated conjecture. The epistemological project, successful application of methodological doubt, therefore, is the most pressing issue for intellectual inquiry.

One more point needs to be made before we turn to the *Meditations*. As remarked earlier, when you read each of the six meditations, or even the excerpts quoted from them in the following chapters, you must read as if you are the author of each meditation or part thereof, as if you are Descartes. Every time you read the word 'I' it must refer to you, not to Descartes. Otherwise you will not really understand what Descartes was doing. His project was neither to articulate his points for himself nor to present them to others as his own contentions; he was, in effect, writing a do-it-yourself guide that everyone could follow to establish basic truths for themselves. Therefore, it has to be you that doubts everything that is not clearly and distinctly true. As you read each consecutive meditation, it has to be you that may be dreaming; it has to be you that may be fooled by the evil spirit; it has to be you who understands that in the very act of doubting your existence you are demonstrating your existence. If you read the *Meditations* in the third person, you will never feel their philosophical power or fully understand what Descartes thought he was achieving in thinking his way through each one. As for this book, in the following chapters on the six meditations, I am careful always to refer to Descartes in the present tense in order to give the material a more immediate tone. You need to feel immediacy as you read and to engage with the material as you would with important current events. Do not read what follows, much less the *Meditations*, as history. You will not fully appreciate Descartes' thought if you only read about it; you need to do it.

SUMMARY

Just as rereading is strongly recommended, some repetition is advisable in order for you to get clear on what are, after all, positions and arguments that are of some difficulty and presumably are new to you. It will prove useful, then, to recapitulate the most important of the foregoing points. I proceed by reiterating the basics and then listing their pluses and minuses in order for you to begin reading about the first meditation in as informed a way as possible.

Descartes sets out to ground human knowledge on absolute certainty. He does so for its own sake, but also to insure that there never again would be occasion for errors to prompt challenges to and revisions of established knowledge. To ground knowledge on certainty, he begins by doubting everything he can doubt, seeking even a single truth he cannot doubt because of its evidency: its clarity and distinctness. Once he has one indubitable truth, he can rebuild his beliefs by comparing their constituents to that one truth. In his view, the same procedure will allow us to develop human knowledge to its fullest extent.

On the plus side, Descartes' philosophical thought was as innovative and productive as his mathematics in that he offered a persuasive presentation of skeptical analytic methodology and thereby prioritized reason in a novel and productive way. Descartes' thought was also innovative in providing a new conception of consciousness and its contents, a conception that greatly influenced the development of empiricism and through it Anglo-European philosophy down to our own time. And Descartes' thought was innovative in providing a fresh causal argument for the existence of God.

On the minus side, Descartes' philosophical thought failed to apply methodological doubt as rigorously as he set out to do. His thought incorporates several problematic assumptions and presuppositions, the most notable being: failure to reflect on language's role in the shaping of thought; facile acceptance of memory's reliability in philosophical arguments; unreflective acceptance of the concept of substance; and ambiguity in his conception of ideas.

It is now time to turn to the first meditation.

CHAPTER 3

THE FIRST MEDITATION: METHODOLOGICAL DOUBT

We can now proceed with an outline of the structure of the first meditation's argument. After some preliminaries, Descartes sets out to doubt the evidence of his senses: he notes that everything he believes 'has been acquired from the senses or by means of the senses' but has learned that his senses sometimes deceive him (Descartes 1, 18 [I, 145]).

Having sometimes failed him, Descartes' senses are now suspect because past errors show that there is nothing about individual instances of sensory perception that is self-verifying, and therefore there can be no certainty gained through our senses. At this stage, sensory perception has not yet been reduced to ideas occurring in the mind, and questions have not yet been raised about whether those ideas are veridical in having objective causes. At this stage, Descartes is emulating an approach that dates back to the skepticism of philosophers such as Pyrrho (360–270 BCE) and Sextus Empiricus (*circa* 200). The tactic is to recall cases in which he has misperceived something and to then generalize on that basis that the senses are not to be trusted. This is to sacrifice the huge bulk of reliable perception because of a relatively small possibility of error, but it is a tactic that was shown effective more than a thousand years before Descartes employed it. But more important than Descartes' emulation of skeptics like Pyrrho is his tacit acceptance of what the emulation entails, which is the quintessentially Platonic conception of knowledge as absolute, certain, and unchanging.

What you need to see to appreciate the point being made here is that skeptics from Pyrrho to Descartes and beyond invariably gloss the difference between perceptual error and what I will describe as interpretive latitude in sensory perception. What I mean is that often problematic perceptions are not so much wrong as ambiguous or indeterminate. Take a simple case: you see someone at a distance and are not sure if it is a friend or a stranger. This is not a case of being deceived by your sense of sight but of not being sure for lack of detail. Again, railroad tracks seem to converge at a distance. This, too, is not a case of visual deception; it is a matter of perspective that fools no one. A rare nonvisual example of skeptical doubt goes back to Sextus Empiricus and is that tepid water feels cool to someone who has been exercising but feels warm to someone who has been at rest. These are not perceptual errors, but they are used to conclude that the senses cannot provide us with certainty. As Plato would put it, they yield only 'opinion,' not knowledge.

Descartes takes the skeptical tactic further to achieve greater scope by supposing that perhaps he is dreaming and that everything that he sees, hears, feels, tastes, and smells actually is the content of a dream and not real at all. His aim is to impugn his own faith in sensory perception in a systematic way by moving from occasional perceptual error to holistic illusion. He wants to establish that however real things may feel, look, sound, taste, and smell, there is always a slight but nonetheless real possibility that they are all illusory.

Most of us have had the experience of waking from a vivid dream and being surprised by the sudden dissolution of one range of experiences and the onset of another. Descartes' proposal does not strike us as bizarre as it might, and he is, of course, counting on precisely that reaction. His main point does seem fair enough: Descartes' claim is that 'there are no conclusive indications by which waking life can be distinguished from sleep' (Descartes 1, 19 [I, 146]). What is more problematic is how far he presses his point, which is to the implausible possibility that we actually may be dreaming or hallucinating or otherwise deluded at any given time regardless of context and the vividness of our awareness. He needs to press the point that far because his aim is to impugn sensory perception as a whole.

There is a more subtle alternative reading of Descartes' dream argument that merits mention, not only because it may be what Descartes in fact intends, but also because it illustrates the complexity of philosophical interpretation. It has been argued that rather than challenging our ability to distinguish dreaming and waking states, Descartes is maintaining that we have no reason to believe that effects resemble their causes in the waking state, since they clearly do not do so in the dreaming state (Wilson 1978).

The point of this interpretation is that we are no better off when awake than when dreaming when it comes to determining with exactness that the perceptions we have faithfully represent their causes. This is not so much a matter of perceptual error as it is of radical doubts that the world in itself actually is as we perceive it. This interpretation has the advantage of making better sense of Descartes' retraction in the sixth meditation, when he tells us that temporal coherence does enable us to tell apart waking and dreaming states. This interpretation also is consistent with the above-quoted passage, because the point of the claim about no conclusive way to tell waking from dreaming states would be not so much that dreaming states are wholly deceptive, as that there is nothing about waking states that guarantees the representative accuracy of sensory perception.

The trouble is that despite a measure of plausibility outside of an epistemological context, we find it hard to really think that while fully awake we might nonetheless be dreaming. We can accept that we might be deluded about a particular sensory perception, but it is Descartes' contention that all of our waking experience might be a dream; that is what we find difficult to take seriously. Still, we are forced to admit the logical possibility that regardless of how vivid our waking experience might be, we could really awaken in the next moment.

What admitting the logical possibility means is only that it is not self-contradictory to say: 'Even though I am certain that I am awake, I could at this moment actually be asleep and dreaming.' To support the point, we can readily substitute some other condition for being asleep and dreaming, such as being under the influence of one or another drug. The point, then, is just this: we must allow that at any moment our ongoing experience might change so radically that what preceded the change is judged to have been illusory. This essentially is what Descartes wants us to admit, and it is difficult to see how we could refuse to do so. The question is, though, whether admitting the logical possibility is enough for Descartes' purposes. The trouble is that Descartes' methodological doubt requires actual doubt about our awareness, and admission of the logical possibility of systematic error is a long way from actual doubt.

Assuming acceptance of Descartes' hypothesis that we might be dreaming at any given time, even if only as a logical possibility, it may seem that he has all he needs to clear his mind of everything which can be doubted and so is prepared to recognize whatever he may be aware of that is indubitable and undeniably true. Given his hypothesis that perhaps everything we are aware of is illusory, it looks as if whatever stands out as a totally undoubtable object of thought must be true, and if there is something that is undoubtable, he will have the sample of absolute truth his methodology requires. However, the dream hypothesis by itself is not enough to generate the thoroughgoing philosophical doubt Descartes needs, quite aside from our reservations about the difference between logical possibility and actual doubt. Why it is not enough is clear as soon as we realize that even if we systematically doubt our sensory perception because of the dream hypothesis, that hypothesis does not force or even call for doubting of our reason. This point, taken together with Descartes' understanding of reason as itself a source of beliefs, means that for his methodological doubt to work, he needs also to impugn reason as a source of beliefs.

The inadequacy of the dream hypothesis is that even if we admit that we may be being systematically deceived by our senses, we may feel quite certain about a number of things, such as that five plus five equals ten or that a triangle must have internal angles equaling 180 degrees. These are truths the denials of which are contradictions, so they do not admit of even the logical possibility of being false.

The shortfall in the dream hypothesis is that it does not impugn truths which are not affected by being possibly only dreamt as opposed to grasped in waking life. In the case of five plus five equaling ten, for instance, whether I really add five and five, hallucinate the addition while awake, or only dream the addition, it remains true that five plus five equals ten. Descartes needs to impugn even these truths, the so-called 'truths of reason,' which seem to be evidently true even in dreams. Surely, then, these truths provide the keystone truths Descartes needs to test other apparent truths – or can Descartes' methodological doubt impugn even truths of reason?

What Descartes does to carry through his wholesale questioning of everything he believes is to imagine that beyond the possibly systematic deception of his senses postulated in the dream hypothesis, there is a very powerful and malevolent entity, the 'evil spirit,' that just as systematically deceives Descartes regarding the truths of reason: 'I will . . . suppose that . . . a certain evil spirit . . . has bent all his efforts to deceiving me' (Descartes 1, 22 [I, 148]). If Descartes believes that five plus five equals ten, then, it is because the evil spirit makes him believe it, and Descartes' inability to see how five plus five could equal, say, twelve, is also due to the evil spirit's machinations.

At this juncture it is important to your understanding of Descartes in particular, and of philosophy in general, that you stop and think about Descartes' evil-spirit ploy. If you find yourself having reservations about the idea, even if you are not sure why, you are beginning to appreciate the nature of the Cartesian exercise and you are also beginning to develop philosophical instincts. The evil-spirit hypothesis does raise questions. What escapes many who read Descartes for the first time is what I will describe as the object-oriented nature of the evil-spirit hypothesis. By 'object-oriented' I mean that the dream hypothesis is about the objects of thought, not about thought itself. The evil-spirit hypothesis is narrowly about the truths of reason, not about reason or reasoning.

Contemporaries new to Descartes tend to take it that what Descartes' evil spirit impugns is reason in the sense of the process of reasoning, but this is not so. If the evil-spirit hypothesis were about reasoning itself, Descartes could not proceed with his search for truth, for he would face the impossible task of explaining how his reasoning about truth, the existence of God, his own existence, and the existence of the world, could succeed despite the evil spirit's distortions. But the problem does not arise for Descartes because he does not focus on reasoning but on its products due to the nature of his conception of thought.

Recall that Descartes thinks of thinking as the entertaining of ideas, and as becomes evident in the work of the empiricists who followed, especially Locke and Hume, this is an inherently passive conception of thought. The empiricists, and most explicitly Hume, cast thinking and reasoning as manipulation and comparison of ideas, and have very little to say about just what the manipulation itself consists of other than speaking generally about compilation, division, and comparison. Neither Descartes nor the empiricists explain how thinking produces ideas; they understand thinking as dealing with ideas that are present to the mind, and the only question that concerns them about the sources of the ideas is whether or not the ideas have external causes and so are or are not representations of something other than themselves. It was not until Kant that a more sophisticated and active conception of thinking and reasoning was introduced.

Given Descartes' understanding of the nature of thought, the evil-spirit hypothesis is really a hypothesis about the external source of ideas; a hypothesis that attributes all ideas to the evil spirit and thereby renders them all deceptive. What Descartes really succeeds in doing when he applies the evil-spirit hypothesis, therefore, is to make problematic the ideas he considers the objects of reason, as he makes problematic the ideas he considers objects of sensory perception when he applies the dream hypothesis. The evil spirit does not distort reasoning itself.

The significance of the foregoing is that regardless of his claim to doubt everything of which he is not absolutely certain, Descartes never doubts his ability to reason – that is, his capacity to think discursively and to do so effectively. Neither the dream hypothesis nor the evil-spirit hypothesis impugns Descartes' reasoning; they impugn only the ideational contents of his mind. His methodological doubt, then, is not as thoroughgoing as he intends it to be and contends it is.

The fact is that if Descartes impugned his ability to reason, he simply could not go further than the first meditation; he would remain a skeptic of the early Greek variety, his philosophical contribution being limited to the claim that nothing can be known. Postulation of the evil spirit should preclude that any reasoning which follows the postulation could yield reliable reasoned conclusions, but Descartes does not allow that to happen, not because he is being disingenuous, but because his conception of thought limits the evil spirit to impugning only ideas, only the objects of thought.

* * *

As we have seen, what Descartes takes himself to be doing is doubting everything in order to clear away every belief that is in any way problematic. He thinks that if he succeeds in his methodological doubt, then anything that remains as an object of thought and which he cannot doubt must be true, and that once he finds even one such truth, he will know what truth is like. He will then be able to use the discovered instance of truth as a sample for testing other beliefs, and those that match the sample in clarity and distinctness will also be indubitably true.

Descartes fails to apply methodological doubt to his own reasoning, by not wondering, for instance, whether he in fact can reliably compare true and potentially true ideas as he sets out to do. But aside from this failure, Descartes' thinking about finding a sample of truth and checking other beliefs against it is surprisingly naive. He assumes that recognizing his sample of truth is like seeing something which he will always be able to identify when he sees it again because of its clarity and distinctness, and so that it will serve as a dependable basis for comparison. What enables him to think in this way, to feel sure of his ability not only to recognize truth but to use it comparatively, is that he thinks of truth as a distinct and separate property of ideas. The significance of this is that as a property, truth essentially is something that an idea either has or fails to have, so that recognition of an idea as true really is awareness of the idea and of its property of being true. The question this immediately should raise in your mind is this: if there are clear and distinct truths at all, especially ones as imposing as Descartes makes out, why is methodological doubt necessary to discern them?

Why is it necessary to go through the doubting exercise to recognize the property of truth possessed by the most basic and fundamental truths? Should not clear and distinct truths stand out on their own among those we only hold true, regardless of how fervently we may hold the latter?

The implication in Descartes' whole approach is that problematic and false ideas and beliefs somehow manage to obscure even fundamental clear and distinct truths, at least enough that methodological doubt is necessary. The result is a picture that looks something like this: the mind is cluttered with ideas, just as a trunk may be filled with odds-and-ends. Applying methodological doubt is like going through the things in the trunk and deciding which are worth keeping and which should be thrown away. In the same way, we recognize value in some of the things in the trunk, we recognize truth in some of the ideas and beliefs in our mind. However, this seems to happen only when we actively doubt or try to doubt each idea or belief, as when we set out to go through the things in a trunk for something of value. The significance of this picture is that it seems that clarity and distinctness can be occluded, despite all we are told about their evidence in the light of reason.

Recall once more the importance of visual metaphors in Descartes' thinking. Once you do so, you understand better how he models recognition of truth on visual recognition, but you also see more clearly the problems reliance on the visual raises. In fairness to Descartes, his reliance on visual metaphor in the conception of thought is not as simplistic as some portray it. Critics of Descartes who stress his reliance on the visual tend to cast his conception of thought in overly simple terms because their intent is to emphasize a more complex juxtaposition of subject and object than is allowed for in Descartes' picture of the mind and its contents. Admittedly, Descartes does say things that support the critics; he tells us that his thoughts 'are like images of objects, and it is to these alone that the name of "idea" properly applies' (Descartes 3, 35–36 [I, 159]). The critics criticize this conception for reifying the objects of awareness into so many image-like ideas, but while there is a good deal of truth to this criticism, the real problem with Descartes' reliance on visual metaphors is what was alluded to earlier, which is that objects of awareness, as image-like ideas, become representations of their causes and cease to be the objects of sensory perception themselves. This makes the world disappear into an inferred realm to which we have access only through the ideas the world causes in our minds, and it then becomes necessary to establish that our ideas have external causes and so are representations rather than 'internal' products of imagination or the like.

It is important to appreciate the theological underpinnings of Descartes' methodological doubt and how they allow him to go as far as he does with the dream hypothesis and especially the evil-spirit hypothesis. The theological doctrine underlying methodological doubt is not only that everything that exists is the result of divine will, but that further, everything that can be conceived, such as five plus five equaling ten, is the result of divine will. Five plus five equaling ten is not due to something inherent in numbers themselves, or in arithmetic as an autonomous phenomenon or as a defined closed system, but because God wills it to be so.

The very possibility of the evil-spirit hypothesis has two theological presuppositions. One is that God may tolerate the evil spirit as He tolerates Satan, perhaps only as a source of temptation. The other presupposition is that the evil spirit can make even the most apparently obvious idea or belief, such as five and five making ten, be deceptive because there is no necessity outside of what God wills to be so. We may not understand how five plus five could equal anything other than ten, but God could have made it so, and therefore the evil spirit is capable of deceiving us. Differently put, logic is not autonomous; in effect, God determines what is or is not logical. In this, Descartes likely was inspired by the theology of Augustine (354–440), wherein divine will is totally supreme, as opposed to by that of Thomas Aquinas (1225–1274), in which logic or rationality seems to be autonomous. The evil spirit, then, appears not to be bound by the law of noncontradiction. (The law of noncontradiction bars assertion of both P and not-P, where 'P' is any proposition capable of being true or false, on pain of incoherence.) The import of this is that because there are no logical limitations on the evil spirit, the spirit is apparently not limited in how it may deceive Descartes. As we will see in the next chapter, though, there is a limit to the evil spirit's power to deceive, though whether the limit is consistent with Descartes' initial postulation is one of the many questions you must consider as you proceed with your reading of this book and the *Meditations*.

*   *   *

In the first meditation, then, Descartes sets out to clear his mind of everything that can possibly be doubted, convinced that he will be left with at least one instance of indubitable truth that will stand out in isolation and provide him with a criterion for judging every other idea or belief he has or may acquire. If he succeeds in his methodological doubt, not only will he have a sample of indubitable truth, he will have bedrock on which he can ground the knowledge that he may find he possesses and that he may later achieve.

In proceeding as he does, Descartes talks readily about systematically taking up a doubtful attitude toward everything he has believed up to this point in his life, but it is an appropriate and serious question just how realistic it is to try to doubt what one has no reason to doubt – especially the reality of one's own body. Descartes realized the implausibility of what he is suggesting, which is why he introduces the dream and the evil-spirit hypotheses. But these hypotheses tend to beg the question (in the original sense of assuming what they are supposed to show – from the Latin *petitio principi* – rather than in the present-day sense of simply raising a question). That is, neither the dream nor the evil-spirit hypothesis really changes anything; each is, in fact, no more than a kind of metaphor for thoroughgoing doubt, and it is precisely the possibility of thoroughgoing doubt that is at issue. Descartes simply fails to really address the question of whether we can genuinely doubt what we have no practical reason to doubt. Yet it is absolutely crucial to his enterprise that we be able to doubt what we most firmly believe, since without doing so we are unable to continue with Descartes' philosophical project.

It will prove useful to make explicit here what is only implicit in my speaking of genuine doubt. We are dealing with three different levels of doubt in trying to understand Descartes' methodology, only one of which is at issue in Descartes' dream and evil-spirit hypotheses. First, there is a kind of lip-service doubt, where

60

someone reading the *Meditations* might admit, perhaps somewhat dismissively, that it is logically possible – not contradictory – to say while awake that we might be dreaming or deceived by the evil spirit. But this level of doubt is inadequate for Descartes' purposes, as it does not prompt serious enough investigation or review of what we accept as true. Second, there is what I am calling genuine doubt, which – if we can actually achieve it – involves taking the dream and evil-spirit hypotheses seriously enough to earnestly examine even our most ordinary and apparently evident beliefs and perceptions. Third, there is real or practical, behavior-altering doubt, which is uncalled for and could be or become pathological. This is a dangerous overreaction to Descartes' hypotheses and not conducive to his purposes. Putting things this way makes clearer how important and elusive is the called-for second sort of genuine doubt, and sharpens our reservations about whether Descartes' hypotheses can, in fact, induce the right sort of questioning of our beliefs and perceptions.

* * *

So far we have Descartes introducing his methodological doubt, relying on the dream and evil-spirit hypotheses without adequately considering the possibility of effectively doubting the obvious. His goal is to discover one or more basic truths wholly impervious to doubt, and to do that he has to be able to doubt everything, since otherwise the indubitable character of one or a few truths will not be established beyond possible question.

We now have to distance ourselves a little from the introduction of methodological doubt and have a closer look at what underlies it, which is Descartes' basic conviction that knowledge must be grounded on self-evident basic truths and that it is possible to so ground knowledge. This defining characteristic of Cartesian thought entails that knowledge is hierarchical, that complex truths are based on and composed of simpler truths. Descartes' hierarchical view of knowledge further entails that a belief cannot be judged to be knowledge until it has been analyzed into its various components and each of those components individually tested for truth. This latter point is the heart of Descartes' emphasis on analysis and a major aspect of what made his philosophizing modern.

Unfortunately, while Descartes' emphasis on analysis is all to the good, his application of it raises problems regarding the objectives he thinks achievable.

There are two related problems. First, on Descartes' view, when we get to bedrock, when we reach the simplest and most fundamental truths, we supposedly reach truths that are and can only be their own justification. We supposedly reach truths that are not themselves capable of being further corroborated or confirmed because they are ultimate and self-verifying; they are truths that serve as their own conclusive evidence for their own veracity. This, of course, entails a Platonic understanding of truth as wholly objective and unchanging, because only if truth is unchanging and wholly objective can it be unconditional and it must be unconditional to be self-verifying.

The second problem is that in Descartes' thinking self-evident truths are and must be immediately and evidently present to the mind as true, and given his conception of the mind and consciousness, self-evident truths are ideas presented to the mind as true. However, it is difficult to understand how ideas can be present to the mind as evidently true. The root of this second problem is that for Descartes, the linguistic is once removed from immediately evident truths because it is propositional rendition or articulation of ideas. For him, then, what presents itself to the mind as self-evidently true is at least initially nonlinguistic. We have, therefore, a picture of some ideas being presented to the mind as self-verifying representations of certain ultimacies that we can only think of as Platonic in the sense of being states of being or states of affairs that are absolute. The second problem, then, has two aspects: one is how we are to understand ideas as true in themselves, as representations that are indubitable portraits of the ultimacies that cause them; the other is how we are to understand the nature of those ultimacies.

With a view to your appreciation of the broader contemporary philosophical context, I mention briefly in connection with the two problems just considered that the notion that nonlinguistic ideas present to the mind can confirm or justify beliefs is now almost universally rejected. Donald Davidson, one of the most important philosophers of our time, maintains that 'nothing can count as a reason for holding a belief except another belief' (Davidson 1986, 310). Davidson adds that 'knowledge depend[s] on experience, and experience ultimately [depends] on sensation. But this is the "depend[s]" of causality, not of evidence or justification' (Davidson 1986, 313–14).

Davidson's point applies to Descartes in the following way. Descartes basically confuses causality and justification in thinking that self-verifying ideas – ideas that are present to the mind as guaranteed to be true representations – ground or verify beliefs. The trouble is, again, his reliance on the visual. Descartes' is thinking of the having of a self-verifying idea on the model of seeing that something is the case, as when we confirm that a friend's car is red, say, by looking at the car. But this picture of justification glosses the difference between the mere sight of a red car, which is the causal aspect, and seeing that our friend's car is red, which is the justificatory aspect. Just experiencing the color, just seeing the red car, does not justify the propositional belief or claim that our friend's car is red because the sensory perception of the car's color is not, in itself, confirmation of anything. We have to formulate a proposition to the effect that our friend's car is, indeed, red – whether or not we actually articulate it. Davidson's point is that more must go on for sensory perception of the car's red color to be an observation and so confirmation or justification of the claim or belief that our friend's car is red. Differently put, that the red car we are looking at is our friend's car cannot be packed into the mere sensory image of the car.

What is most basically at issue here is that it is not clear precisely what a Cartesian self-evident nonpropositional truth could be; it is not clear how an idea presented to the mind can be evidently true if truth is not propositionally attributed to the idea. What is missing in Descartes' conception of (some) ideas as evidently true in themselves is understanding that something presented to consciousness is not, as mere sensory content of which we are aware, an object of cognition or reflective awareness. Before sensory content can be an object of cognition or reflective awareness, it must first be conceptualized, interpreted; it must be brought under some concept so that the sensory content can be perception of a particular thing or event or situation. Descartes, and the empiricists who follow him, proceed as if mere presentation of an idea or image, the simple having of sensory content, is having a thought. This understanding of thought will not work because it leaves out the necessary role of conceptualization. Admittedly, it was not until Kant that we began to understand conceptualization and how it is a precondition of cognition, but the point here is not to criticize Descartes anachronistically; the point is for you to better understand what Descartes is contending and the questions his contentions raise.

SUMMARY

To close this consideration of the first meditation, we can sum things up as follows: in the first meditation Descartes attempts to clear the way for discernment of indubitable truth by doubting everything he can doubt. He uses the dream and evil-spirit hypotheses to cast doubt on the evidence of his senses and on truths of reason. Implicit in his approach is the conviction that to gain knowledge, we must analyze our beliefs into their simplest components and test each of those components by comparing them to self-evident truths. Once we have done that, we must reassemble the components that pass the test for truth into the complex beliefs we began with, or approximations of them if we found false components in our analyses and tests for truth.

What we compare belief-components to are truths we have discerned through application of methodological doubt and discerned as self-evidently true. These are ideas that present themselves to us as clear and distinct through the light of reason. Only when the process of analysis, comparison, and verification has been successfully completed can we judge something we believe or are inclined to believe to be true belief and hence knowledge, and only when something is judged knowledge can it be used to test other beliefs. The process is cumulative, in that as we proceed we are adding incrementally to our knowledge and thereby enabling acquisition of further knowledge.

At the end of the first meditation Descartes is poised to consider whether his most important and deep-seated beliefs – about his own existence, about God's existence, about the world's existence – are true. What he needs to proceed is a single self-evidently true idea that will serve as his standard for testing the components of all of his beliefs. And though the point remains unspoken, Descartes' need of a single self-evidently true idea also is a need to establish that his conception of truth is correct.

CHAPTER 4

THE SECOND MEDITATION: THE *COGITO*

The intricacy of the underlying structure of the argument of the second meditation is greater than what we encountered in the first meditation. This is because what the second meditation argues is considerably more complex in conception than is methodological doubt, regardless of the latter's novelty. Assuming that you are following the advice given in Chapter 1 on how to read this book and the *Meditations*, you will have read the second meditation before starting this chapter. On this assumption, we can proceed with a discussion of the *cogito* argument that is more focused than was our discussion of methodological doubt in Chapter 1, which did not presuppose familiarity with the first meditation. We can begin directly with a critical outline of Descartes' argument and describe the problems his argument poses as we proceed.

* * *

Basically, in the second meditation Descartes derives the idea of an existent, autonomous mind from his undeniable experience of thinking and doubting. In other words, the very doubting that is initiated in the first meditation is used in the second meditation to demonstrate, not only the obvious reality or existence of the doubting itself, and hence of ongoing thinking, but also the presumed existence of the mind that is doing the thinking and doubting. However, the main reason for the complexity is that Descartes does not see the demonstration of the existence of thinking and doubting and of the thinking and doubting mind as two separate steps. As you will see, he thinks that in demonstrating the former, he thereby demonstrates the latter.

The mechanics of the establishment of the existence of a thinking thing, of a doubting mind, turn on Descartes' understanding of thought as a property; that is, what enables him to proceed as he does is his understanding of thought as not itself substantial and therefore as existing only as a property of something that is substantial. Moreover, Descartes understands thought not only as a property, but as the defining property of whatever substance it is a property of – that is, of mind.

The argument essentially is that if there is thought, if there is thinking and doubting, there is some substance that is doing the thinking and doubting. For Descartes, thought conceived of as a property entails that there is something of which it is a property, and that something is a mind. Initially you might wonder why this needs to be said or what could be problematic about assuming it, but Hume, for one, saw no reason why thinking entailed a thinking mind, a thinker different from the thinking. He was quite willing to accept that thought, which for him was the having and manipulating of impressions and ideas, could occur entirely on its own without entailing anything other than occurrent impressions and ideas. Hume did not see the necessity of postulating something in which thoughts occur, a mind distinct from sequences of thoughts; more than that, he saw postulation of a mind as unjustified, given that the occurrence of thought is the only reason Descartes assumes the existence of a mind and, according to Hume, there is nothing about impressions and ideas, nothing about thought, that requires existence of anything else. Against this, Descartes cannot conceive of thought as existing on its own; he takes it as given that thought is and must be a property of something, and that that something is a mind which is distinct from its contents.

* * *

Descartes' conviction that thought entails a thinking mind is what enables him to argue as follows: in doubting one's own existence, if one reflects on the very act of doubting, which is an instance of thinking, one realizes that doubting, in particular, or thinking in general, entails what we can for the moment call occurrent existence: that is, the thinking/doubting exists as it is taking place. Hume would grant Descartes this much; if there is thinking or doubting going on, there is – there exists – thinking or doubting.

But Descartes' conclusion goes considerably further; for him, the existence of thinking or doubting, realized in the reflective awareness of thinking or doubting, is not just awareness that thought is taking place. Descartes immediately concludes that since – in his view – thought cannot exist on its own, the thinking the existence of which is realized in reflective awareness must be the thinking of a substantive mind. If there is thinking going on, there necessarily must be a mind of which the thinking is a property.

Descartes goes further still; he goes beyond positing a mind that exists while thought is taking place. For him, the occurrent existence of thought entails the existence of a mind, but the mind's existence is not itself merely occurrent and transient. Though apparently unaware that it is a third distinct conclusion, following the conclusions about the occurrent existence of thought and the existence of a thinking mind, Descartes concludes that the thinking mind persists and is independent of any particular act of thinking. It follows, as Hume would not allow, that mind exists even when no thought is taking place; that mind exists between thoughts.

Even if Hume allowed Descartes that thinking is a property of a mind, despite seeing no reason to conclude that thinking requires that there be a separate mind doing the thinking, Hume would not accept that the existence of the mind doing the thinking is independent of particular thoughts. But this is precisely what Descartes believes is demonstrated by reflective awareness that thinking is taking place: occurrent thought entails a thinking mind, and a thinking mind, being a substance, exists independently of any given occurrent thought. We have quickly gone from the realization that in wondering if we exist, we think, and so that our thought exists, to concluding that as we wonder if we exist we demonstrate our existence as thinking substances.

* * *

It is important for beginners to appreciate that the substantial mind Descartes believes he has shown must exist if there is thinking, is not identical with an embodied mind. The mind that Descartes believes must exist if there is thinking is a pure mind. Whatever errors Descartes may make in concluding that thinking entails a thinking substance, he does not come close to concluding that that thinking substance is embodied, as that would be to also conclude that extended matter exists. In fact, it is precisely Descartes' care in not concluding that the thinking mind he concludes must exist is an embodied mind that effects the Cartesian division of persons into substantial minds and – possibly existent – material bodies.

What makes the thinking mind substantial – a distinct, autonomous substance – is that it does not exist only when thought is taking place; its substantiality is due to its capacity to think, and realization of that capacity, not to the mind being embodied. What Descartes takes as established in the second meditation is that the mind is not identical with any given thought or set of thoughts, but rather is something which has thoughts. The essential point is that a mind is not a property of anything; it is a substance capable of itself having properties, and as a substance, its defining property is thought.

Stressing that the substantive mind is not an embodied mind is necessary for two different reasons. First, some contemporary readers of the *Meditations* might miss the point because of unfamiliarity with the conception of the mind as an autonomous immaterial substance. Second, it is most important to appreciate how it is in the second meditation that Descartes in effect introduces the absolute distinction between mind and body that generates the position of Cartesian dualism (See Glossary). Admittedly the mind/ body distinction is at least as old as Plato, but it is in Descartes that we find its most uncompromising and unqualified expression. As you will see in the chapters that follow, especially in Chapter 10, the implications of Descartes sharp distinction between mental and physical substances carries momentous implications for epistemology.

* * *

Let us now look more closely at what Descartes thinks he establishes in the second meditation. The point of departure is that the most basic belief Descartes has is in his own existence: that he exists. This belief, therefore, is the primary candidate for methodological doubt, both because of its fundamentality and because it is the likeliest to turn out to be undoubtable and so the likeliest to constitute the required sample of indisputable, self-evident truth.

What Descartes does basically is to offer a reconstruction of the obvious; that is, he does no more than point out that so long as one is thinking, one exists as a thinker. Even at this initial stage, Descartes goes beyond what some, Hume, for instance, would allow. It can be argued that the most Descartes can conclude is that thought is taking place. In any case, he believes that one must exist to think, and takes it that reflection on the point provides him with what he most seeks: a sample of incontrovertible truth. Descartes articulates this truth in his famous – one might say notorious – *cogito* (Latin for 'I am thinking' or 'I think'). He tells us: '*I am, I exist*, is necessarily true every time that I pronounce it or conceive it in my mind' (Descartes 2, 24 [I, 150]). The very act of thinking demonstrates existence. In methodologically doubting his own existence, Descartes is thinking, and in thinking he demonstrates his own existence. Not even the evil spirit can make it so that Descartes is deceived that he exists while he doubts his existence, while he thinks.

Two *caveats*: first, note that the passage quoted in the foregoing paragraph already makes reference to mind. Second, do not confuse the constraint on the evil spirit with a limitation of our finite imagination, and so as something that still allows a margin for deception. That is, do not think that it is just a matter of our being unable to imagine how the evil spirit could make Descartes not exist while he doubts his own existence. The point is that for Descartes to not exist while thinking, and to be deceived about his existence, would be for Descartes to both exist and not exist at the same time, and that is a logical contradiction, not merely something very difficult to imagine. There is simply nothing that could count as both existing – in order to be thinking that one might not exist – and not existing at the same time. Having said this, recall the power attributed to the evil spirit and my point about being deceived regarding five and five equaling ten. The question does arise why logic limits the evil spirit with respect to existence but not with respect to a truth of reason. It is certainly arguable that trying to think how five and five might not equal ten is not so different from trying to imagine how one might be thinking yet not exist.

To proceed, we can put aside speculation about logical limitations and consider more pressing questions raised by Descartes' claim. For instance, something Descartes never considers is whether he continues to be the numerically identical being while intermittently thinking or doubting over even a short period of time. Hume might point out that if God were to annihilate and recreate Descartes moment after moment, but with all the memories of his previous instantiation, there would be a sense in which, though existent in each instant of thinking or doubting, Descartes would not exist as he concludes he does, which is as a persistently existent mind. Another question has to do with earlier allusion to Descartes' inadequate consideration of memory. Thinking or uttering even as short an observation as 'I think, I am' takes a finite amount of time, so it is possible that when he thinks or utters 'I am' Descartes has already forgotten the 'I think' part, in which case his conclusion either would be inadequately supported or simply be an assertion of his existence. Descartes' indifference to or neglect of language also raises a question, in that he never wonders whether the 'I' in 'I think' refers to the same entity as the 'I' in 'I am.' Here again Hume would point out that there is no conclusive reason to believe that the 'I' in both cases refers to a numerically identical mind.

The foregoing may look like quibbles, at least at this early stage, but as you read more you will see they are not quibbles but rather are indications of serious lapses in supposedly rigorous methodological doubt. You also have to keep in mind that it is Descartes who sets the ground rules: he is searching for indubitable, unquestionable, unchallengeable, evident truth – an exercise that does not allow for lapses or omissions.

* * *

The essential point Descartes is making is that in thinking, and in asserting that he is thinking, he is demonstrating his own existence. It seems, then, that he has found his absolute starting point: a sample of indubitable truth. Assertion of his own existence while he is thinking is absolutely incorrigible; he cannot be wrong because to think is to exist. Descartes tells us explicitly: 'I am, I exist . . . I am now admitting nothing except what is necessarily true' (Descartes 2, 26 [I, 152]). But Descartes packs more into this than he should. While it is true enough that Descartes exists while he is thinking because the thinking entails existence, the thinking does not entail that he exists as a thinking thing, as a mind distinct from the ongoing thinking. This is something that he asserts in the process of stating what is necessarily true, that he exists as he thinks; he tells us, 'I am something real and really existing, but what thing am I? [A] thing which thinks' (Descartes 2, 26 [I, 152]). Descartes makes an illegitimate move by going from the admittedly certain fact that while he thinks, he exists as the occurrent thinking, to his further claim that he is a thing that thinks: that he exists as a thinking thing.

Descartes offers no argument for his move from thinking to thinking thing, relying on what was then received opinion to the effect that thought is a property of substantial minds, and so that when thought exists, a thinking mind exists. Recall, however, that he is not referring to being a thing that thinks in the sense of being an embodied mind. This is a crucial point to remember because his aim is to establish the existence of a substantive but nonmaterial mind. What Descartes is concluding is that he is a mental thing that thinks. The existence of matter is still problematic and its establishment as existent is not attempted until the sixth meditation.

There are two problems with Descartes' ready move from thinking to thinking thing. The illegitimacy of the move is only the first. The second has to do with the metaphysical implications of the move, which are that purely mental substances exist and that thinkers are purely mental substances. This is how Descartes effects the division of mind and body: by – supposedly – demonstrating the existence of mind prior to establishing the existence of body or extended matter.

Descartes has all the warrant he needs to say that thought is taking place when he methodically doubts his own existence, and so he has all the warrant he needs to say that he exists as that thinking. But he does not have warrant to say that the thought that is taking place is a property of some mental thing that thinks. He cannot go from the obvious fact that he is thinking to his claim that he is a thinking thing, because being a thing is not something that is warranted by his realization that thought exists while he doubts his own existence. We may not be able to imagine how thought might occur by itself, as Hume seems to have been able to do, but that does not matter. What is at issue is not what we can imagine, but we can conceive, and Hume exemplifies that we can conceive – there is no contradiction in – thought occurring on its own. Descartes cannot validly conclude that he is a thinking thing just from the obviously true premise that he is thinking. All that Descartes establishes in drawing this invalid conclusion is that, as has been stressed, he assumes that thought is a property, and that as a property, thought must attach to something other than itself, just as weight cannot exist by itself but must always be the weight of something.

It merits mention that Descartes' illegitimate move from thinking to thinking thing is not a simple mistake; it is perfectly natural to construe saying that he exists when he thinks as saying that he exists as a thinking being, as something that is distinct from the thinking and which engages in thought. Most readers of this book and of the *Meditations*, possibly including you, most likely take it as obvious that there cannot be just thought, that if there is thought there must be something that thinks. But we are doing epistemology; the applicable standards are much more rigorous than what seems natural or what most people accept. Strictly speaking, the jump from thinking to thinking thing is an invalid one. Descartes' thinking could be the whole of his existence as an autonomous phenomenon, and not be a property of anything. If we apply his own avowedly precise standards to his conclusions, what his doubting his own existence warrants is affirmation that thinking is taking place and nothing more. If he wants to describe his thinking as his existing, that is acceptable. What is not acceptable is for him to go from the thinking being 'something real and really existing,' to asking 'but what thing am I' and then answering 'a thing which thinks.'

* * *

Descartes' *cogito* raises another issue that many find more elusive than the slide from thinking to thing that thinks. It is of concern to Descartes that establishment of his existence on the basis of his thinking and doubting not be understood as the conclusion of an argument. Thus far I have spoken of Descartes concluding this or that, or drawing this or that conclusion, and further spoken of his conclusion that he is a thing that thinks as invalid. However, Descartes would not accept some of these references to drawn conclusions, at least not regarding his existence, because he does not consider observation of his own thinking as providing a premise on the basis of which he draws an argumentative conclusion – a conclusion following logically from sound premises – about his existence. The reason for this is that Descartes claims to directly intuit his existence in the act of thinking or in the act of doubting that very existence.

What Descartes claims is not really complicated, but many find it elusive; worse still, many think it unimportant, and that is seriously mistaken. The elusiveness or imagined unimportance of Descartes' claim about the *cogito* being an intuition and not an argument is evident in how the *cogito* is invariably rendered when discussed in histories of philosophy, in texts dealing with Descartes' work, or in other books. When stated in Latin, the *cogito* is almost always given as '*Cogito, ergo sum*'; when stated in English, the *cogito* is almost always given as 'I am thinking, therefore I exist' or more commonly as 'I think, therefore I am.'

The *cogito* is rendered as including *ergo* or 'therefore' even in some of the best histories of philosophy and the most sophisticated philosophical treatments of Descartes (Audi 1995, 195; Honderich 1995, 189). But to include *ergo* or 'therefore' is to distort the *cogito* as it is presented and used in the *Meditations*; to include *ergo* is to give the *cogito* as Descartes used it in the four-year earlier *Discourse on Method*. What Descartes actually says in the *Meditations* is just what I quote above: in Latin, he says '*Cogito, sum*,' which translates into English as 'I am thinking, I exist,' or 'I think, I am.' The word '*ergo*' does not occur in the *cogito* as articulated in the *Meditations*, and the word 'therefore' should not be included in English or French or other translations of the relevant passages in the *Meditations*.

Descartes' avoidance of the term *ergo*, 'therefore,' in articulating the *cogito* in the *Meditations* as '*Cogito, sum*' or 'I think, I am' or 'I think, I exist' is that he does not believe that the *cogito* is an argument. Inclusion of *ergo* or 'therefore' turns the phrase 'I think' into a premise and the *sum* or 'I am' or 'I exist' into a conclusion following from that premise. But in the *Meditations* Descartes is adamant that the *cogito* is a direct or immediate intuition, not an argument. The reason is that if the *cogito* were an argument, its evident truth would be compromised to the degree that the conclusion – I am, I exist – in following from the premise would require that the truth of the premise be separately established and the conclusion shown to follow validly. Furthermore, to establish that the conclusion follows validly, there would have to be acknowledgment of a suppressed premise such as 'All things that think exist' because a conclusion cannot follow validly from a single premise.

Descartes' insistence that the *cogito* is an immediate intuition rather than an argument raises again the problem of how ideas present themselves as true. The whole point of calling realization of his existence an intuition is that Descartes wants it to be a single, simple apprehension of indubitable truth. He does not want it to be a truth worked out through step-by-step reasoning. Recognition of necessary existence in the act of thinking must be immediate grasp of an indubitable truth. Descartes' point is that if realization of his existence were a conclusion, an inference based on evidence or premises distinct from the inference itself, the realization could be challenged or might be erroneous, even if it is not obvious how it might be so.

Descartes, then, does not see himself as concluding that since he is thinking, he exists; instead he sees himself as realizing in the very act of thinking – in the very act of doubting his own existence – that in thinking he manifests his existence. Articulation of this intuition, this realization, is necessary only because he is writing out his meditation. In this we see again the secondary place of language in Descartes' thought. Realization of his own existence is integral to his doubting that existence and to thinking generally. Actually saying *cogito, sum* or 'I think, I exist' is necessary only for the sake of others.

Once it is clear how realization of his own existence in thinking is an immediate intuition, it becomes clearer not just how the *cogito* provides Descartes with the sought-for wholly undoubtable truth, but how that undoubtable truth is unitary, instantaneously grasped, and utterly simple in the sense of not having aspects or components. It is, therefore, an evident, undoubtable truth that the dream and evil-spirit hypotheses cannot impugn: dreaming, like thinking, manifests existence and not even the evil spirit can deceive what does not exist.

* * *

As noted, the existence of matter remains to be dealt with. It is important not to lose sight of this point because, again as noted, Descartes does not see his establishing his own existence as a thinking thing as establishing that he is embodied. 'Thinking thing' refers to a substantive mind, not to anything material. As for matter itself, it raises two different issues: one about whether or not it actually exists, which is dealt with in the sixth meditation, and another about its nature or form of existence. Because in the second meditation Descartes takes himself to establish the existence of mind as a substance, he has to address the second issue about matter's nature, even if only in a preliminary manner.

Descartes proceeds on the assumption that he not only has his sample of indubitable truth in the intuition that he exists as a thinker, but that establishing his existence as a thing that thinks establishes the existence of mind as a substance and defines that substance by manifesting its essential property, thought. Descartes then turns to examining his deeply-held belief that there is matter, that he is an embodied mind, with a view to discerning the property that defines matter as he has discerned the property that defines mind.

It is important to appreciate that in the second meditation Descartes does not consider matter as we normally think of it, as the physical stuff of the universe. What Descartes considers is what he calls 'extension.' It is extension that he maintains is what the intellect grasps as the common element in ideas presented to the mind of the objects in the world around us. It is extension, as the common element, that may be real and so be the cause of the ideas. Basically, as thought is the defining property of mind, extension may be the defining property of matter. But the actual existence of extended matter is not at issue in the second meditation; as noted earlier, that is postponed until the sixth meditation. What is at issue in the second meditation is extension as a common element in ideas of purportedly existent material objects. To put the point in contemporary terms, what Descartes considers in the second meditation essentially is the concept of matter, not the existence of matter.

* * *

With respect to proving his own existence, Descartes' thinking and doubting suffice because it is in the very act of thinking or doubting that he demonstrates his existence. He then goes too far, taking it that his intuition about existing as he thinks establishes that he is a thing that thinks. But what is pivotal here is that Descartes sees the assertion that he is a thing that thinks as legitimated by thought being the defining property of mental substance: of a thing that thinks. It is different with matter because its defining property cannot be known directly or immediately, it cannot be experienced 'from the inside,' as we might put it. Matter's defining property needs to be inferred or deduced from what is common to all ideas of material objects. This is where the wax experiment or example comes in.

Descartes concludes from the wax experiment that being extended is the defining property of potentially existent matter or what he then calls extension. But both the nature of the wax experiment and the need for it manifest how the defining property of matter is deduced from a number of comparisons; it is not directly evident. Descartes proceeds by taking a piece of wax and observing it under as many different conditions as possible. He uses wax because it changes markedly when cooled or heated, thereby yielding various different ideas of what is the same object; the same piece of wax is hard and has a definite shape when cold and becomes soft and alters its shape when heated. The point of the experiment is that as Descartes heats and cools a piece of wax, it is clear that despite quite marked changes in shape, odor, sound-emitting properties, and viscosity, all the ideas of the wax have one thing in common: the wax continues to be extended; it continues to be three dimensional – and notice that for reasons explained hereafter, neither Descartes nor I say or can say that the wax in various forms continues to take up space. Descartes' conclusion is that the defining property of the material objects that so many of his ideas are ideas of is extension.

To reiterate, establishing that extension is common to ideas of material objects says nothing about whether the causes of those ideas are existent instances of extended matter. It is possible that when Descartes concludes that extension is the common element of ideas of material objects he is either dreaming or being fooled by the evil spirit. Nothing is proven about matter's existence in the second meditation; it is only the idea of matter as a possibly existent extended substance that is established.

At the end of the second meditation, Descartes concludes that the sequence of appearances of the piece of wax with which he experiments by heating and cooling it is most readily explicable if matter – assuming it exists – continues to be extended regardless of how its form may change. Let us now consider the wax experiment more carefully to better understand how Descartes derives extension as the defining property of matter as a substance.

* * *

Descartes proceeds by looking at a piece of beeswax, noting its irregular shape and white color; he smells it, noting a faint flowery fragrance; he touches it to his tongue and detects a slight honey flavor; he raps it on the table, noting the dull sound it makes; he feels its hard, cool texture, noting its somewhat greasy feel. He then heats the wax and observes how everything he has observed changes. The piece of wax loses its irregular shape and forms a small pool on the table's surface; its odor changes in being intensified; its taste changes in also being intensified; it can no longer be rapped on the table due to its semiliquid state; its texture changes as it becomes soft and warm and the greasy feel of its surface changes from a greasy feel to a slight stickiness.

What Descartes focuses on is that whatever changes the wax undergoes, it continues to be extended – but again, as noted, we cannot say that it continues to be extended in space, as I will explain in a moment. The conclusion Descartes draws is that after heating the wax, what defines it as the same wax is not 'that sweetness of honey, nor that ... odor of flowers, nor that whiteness, nor that shape, nor that sound, but only a body,' but it is a very different body that looks, smells, tastes, and feels unlike the wax before it was heated. Descartes concludes that when we abstract away the changing properties, 'nothing is left but something extended' (Descartes 2, 29–30 [I, 154]).

Note that Descartes speaks of what remains as something extended, saying nothing about the medium in which the thing is extended; that is, he is careful not to say that the piece of wax, in all its various forms, remains extended in space. The reason is intriguing and indicates the sort of complex but often captivating issue that can arise in philosophy. Descartes rejects anything like the Newtonian notion of absolute space – and, of course, he has no understanding of the Einsteinian concept of relative space. For Descartes, the material universe is a plenum: there is no empty space because matter – what is not mind – is a substance defined by extension, as mind is a substance defined by thought. If Descartes were to acknowledge empty space, it would have to be as another substance. But empty space lacks a defining property; for instance, it cannot be defined by emptiness since things take up space. Therefore, empty space is not conceivable as a substance. The only substance other than mind and possibly existent extended matter is God, the divine substance the existence of which is supposedly proven in the third and fifth meditations.

Regardless of how difficult the idea may seem, Descartes is consistent in disallowing the existence of empty space. As for what appears to us as empty space, for him that is simply other forms of extension. For example, air is material, so is extended, despite that it appears to us as emptiness. Descartes goes to some pains to establish that however rarefied stuff might be, as in the case of the subtlest of gasses, it is material; it is extended, and therefore not something that is extended in empty space (Kemp-Smith 1958, 65–73). Descartes does speak of space, as when he speaks of the lines of a geometric figure enclosing a space. However, in these cases he is not speaking of empty space in a Newtonian sense; he is referring only to what is delineated by determinate objects, such as drawn lines forming a triangle. In any case, the significance in the present context of Descartes' conception of the physical world as a plenum is that mind and matter as substances exhaust what there is – aside from God, of course. Moreover, mind is established as existent in virtue of the occurrence of its defining property: thought. And now that Descartes has identified the defining property of matter, extension, he is in a position to establish its existence. However, as we will see in the next chapter and in Chapter 5, establishing the existence of God takes precedence.

It is worth noting, in passing, that the conception of the material world as a plenum actually is not coherent because of motion, of things moving within the hypothetical plenum. Descartes seems to have thought that extended objects displaced one another in moving, but we understand that cannot be. Fortunately or unfortunately, we cannot pursue this arcane issue here; if it intrigues you, I refer you to Norman Kemp-Smith's *Descartes: Philosophical Writings* (Kemp-Smith 1958).

* * *

At the close of the second meditation, Descartes sees himself as having achieved three objectives of paramount importance to his project. First, he has established his own existence – in his view as a thing that thinks, a mental substance. Second, in establishing his own existence through the intuition articulated in the *cogito*, he gets his sample of clear and distinct absolute truth. Third, he discerns the defining property of the possibly existent material objects that cause the ideas that populate his sensory awareness and that he has of his own possibly existent material body. Descartes takes it that methodological doubt and careful analysis have confirmed his most fundamental belief: that of his own existence. Moreover, methodological doubt and careful analysis have put him on the path to confirming an only slightly less fundamental belief: that he is an embodied mind in a world of mind-independent material objects.

With respect to the aforementioned reservations about the first two meditations, and especially about the second, the salient one is how Descartes goes from the undeniable fact that he exists as he thinks or doubts to the problematic assertion that he exists as a thing that thinks, as a mental substance. This is the most worrying move he makes for two reasons: first, it is based only on the presupposition that thought is the defining property of an independent – mental – substance; second, it is the move with the most significant philosophical implications because, if accepted, it establishes a metaphysical difference in kind between the mental and the physical. The long-lived philosophical position resulting from this difference is mind/body dualism.

SUMMARY

Having set up his procedure for discerning truth, namely, methodological doubt, in the first meditation, in the second meditation Descartes establishes – to a greater or lesser degree from our point of view – that he necessarily exists when he thinks; that he is a thing that thinks; and that the ideas he has of material objects, which may or may not exist, enable the derivation of extension as their common defining property. Mind, then, just is that which thinks and which, in thinking, necessarily exists; matter just is that which is extended, and so differs in kind from mind, and which may exist independently of mind.

While the major problem in the first meditation is a procedural one, that is, the credibility of methodological doubt as a workable analytic device, the major problem in the second meditation is metaphysical or ontological in being about the nature of something (See Glossary). The problem also is logical in that Descartes invalidly concludes from the evident reality of his thinking that his thinking is a property and hence that he is a thing that thinks. The only basis for this invalid conclusion is the Aristotelian presupposition that substances have defining properties and Descartes' assumption that thought is the defining property of mental substance. This assumption is also at work in his derivation of extension as the defining property of the ideas he has of material objects, and therefore the defining property of possibly existent matter.

There are, of course, other problems in the second meditation. A general one is his failure to apply methodological doubt as rigorously as he should – for instance, to apply it precisely to his acceptance of the Aristotelian doctrine of substance. There also are issues like that of how nonpropositional ideas present themselves as true. But to again be fair to Descartes, despite difficulties he does advance his project to the extent that he finds he cannot doubt that while he doubts or thinks he exists, and so has found his sought-for sample of indubitable truth. Additionally, he does derive a common essential property of ideas which present themselves to him as material objects: extension.

At the end of the second meditation, Descartes' universe is very limited: it contains only himself, purportedly as a thing that thinks, and allows the possibility that matter exists. He now must intensify his efforts and consider what else he believes firmly that he may establish he actually knows with certainty. Nor is it simply a matter of demonstrating the truth of one or more individual beliefs. Descartes needs to establish the certainty of beliefs in order to enable himself to expand his knowledge; he needs to establish as certain beliefs that, having been proven, will provide the bases for extrapolations to other truths about his world. Despite its huge importance, proof of Descartes' own existence yields only that he exists, and perhaps some support for his contentious claim that he is a mental substance. As for his derivation of extension as the defining property of matter, that remains an open question until he establishes that extended matter actually exists. Descartes' next task, therefore, is to establish the truth of a belief that has important implications for establishing the truth of other beliefs. This is why he devotes the third meditation to proving the existence of God.

CHAPTER 5

THE THIRD MEDITATION: THE CAUSAL ARGUMENT FOR GOD'S EXISTENCE

Descartes begins the third meditation with what amounts to a useful summary of what he thinks he has achieved in the first two meditations. He does this in order to make clear his starting point in reasoning about God's nature and existence, but what he has to say also is of use because it helps us to better understand what Descartes thinks he accomplishes in the first two meditations. He begins by saying he will close his eyes, stop up his ears, and generally disregard his sensory awareness by blocking out or ignoring senses around him, considering all sensory content deceptive. The aim is to isolate what is essential to himself as a thinking mind and to make himself 'better known and more familiar' to himself.

Descartes reiterates that he is a thing that thinks; he exists as a thing that thinks even if only by doubting his own existence and affirming that existence in recognizing that he exists as he thinks. He reflects on the point that if all his ideas, if everything he is aware of is 'nothing at all apart' from himself – that is, is only a product of his own mind, he nonetheless can be certain that all these 'modes of thought,' all the 'sensations and imaginations' he is aware of, 'are found with certainty' in himself 'just as far as they are modes of thought' (Descartes 3, 33 [I, 157]). As ideas present to his mind, the contents of Descartes' awareness are undeniably existent as ideas, even if they have no external causes and are entirely the products of his own imagination.

A number of things are important here. One is that at the end of the second meditation Descartes still has not ventured beyond his own awareness: his own thinking and entertaining of ideas. He is careful to refer to the ideas he has as modes of thought and as possibly nothing more than what he finds in his own mind. Recall that the derivation of extension proves nothing about the independent reality of material objects; it establishes only that if some of Descartes' ideas are of material objects and veridical, the material objects of which he is aware are extended. As for his own existence, that is unquestionable, after the intuition of the *cogito*, but for all he knows, at the end of the second meditation, he – and the ideas he has – are all that exist. This is a position known as solipsism and though Descartes is often accused of being committed to it, it is a position he entertains at the beginning of the third meditation only as a possibility he soon discards (see Glossary).

There is a bit more going on here than Descartes considering that all he can be certain of at this point is his own existence and the actuality of his ideas. The more is what is only implicit in Descartes' review of the contents of his own mind, and that is the unmentioned fact that one of the ideas present in his mind is the idea of God. The unwary reader may take Descartes as only admitting that all his ideas may be no more than the products of his own mind, but what he actually is doing is setting things up to show that the idea of God cannot be a product of his own mind. In strategic terms, the opening of the third meditation does three things: first, it reiterates the certainty of Descartes' existence as a thinking thing; second, it – temporarily – allows the unavoidable possibility that the contents of Descartes' mind may be no more than so many ideas produced by his own mind; and third it surreptitiously prepares the way for Descartes to 'recall' that one of the ideas he has in his mind is that of God.

In terms of what is upfront at the opening of the third meditation, Descartes has examined two of his most fundamental beliefs or ideas: of himself and of the things around him. With respect to himself, he has proven his own existence; with respect to the things around him, he has prepared verification of their existence by deducing their common, defining property. But as noted at the end of the last chapter, he needs to establish something as certain that will enable him to go beyond particular verified beliefs or ideas.

This is where a little subterfuge begins. What he is out to do in the third meditation is prove the existence of God in order to have something to work with that goes beyond individual demonstrated beliefs. The subterfuge is extended when he 'realizes' that among the ideas he has, and which he has just pointed out exist at least as his ideas, there is the idea of God – a very special idea.

* * *

Recall that in order to implement his methodological doubt Descartes uses two devices: the dream hypothesis to render the products of sense-experience questionable, and the evil-spirit hypothesis to render the products of reason questionable. This means that he has established demanding standards with respect to knowledge claims; anything claimed to be known must be capable of proof that is conclusive despite doubts raised by his two hypotheses. To prove the existence of God, therefore, Descartes must rebut his own skepticism by offering arguments that are conclusive in the face of the demands of his methodological doubt. He must, in short, produce arguments with conclusions as certain as his intuition of his own existence, which, after all, is his model of truth. It will not do, with respect to God, to only set the stage for a demonstration of existence as in the case of extended matter. For one thing, if Descartes does not establish the existence of God with certainty, he will not be able to demonstrate the existence of matter because, unlike the proof of his own existence, the proof of the existence of matter must be mediated by something beyond identification of matter's defining property, since matter is known only indirectly through ideas.

What Descartes does is offer a causal argument for the existence of God, an argument which turns on the principle that a cause must be adequate to its effect. His basic strategy is to focus on the idea of God and to show that unlike all his other ideas, the idea of God cannot be a product of his own mind. To achieve this end, Descartes trades on a principle deriving from early Greek thought to the effect that nothing can come from nothing – that is, nothing can come to exist without an adequate cause. He does this just as he traded on the Aristotelian doctrine of substance to establish his own existence as a thing that thinks. The principle Descartes uses was central to Scholastic thought in the medieval period and was rendered in Latin as *ex nihilo nihil fit*: 'from nothing, nothing comes.'

The *ex nihilo* principle holds that whatever causes something to exist must have as much reality, as much potency, as what it imparts to what it causes in causing it to exist. Whether or not this principle makes sense to us, in the context of contemporary scientific knowledge, is an interesting question but one too complex to pursue here. The important point is that Descartes – again falling short in methodological doubt – takes as unproblematic the early Greek and Scholastic doctrine of requisite adequacy of cause to effect to formulate his argument for God's existence.

The causal argument Descartes offers briefly is that the only possible source of the idea of God is God himself, because no other cause can be adequate to produce the idea of God. Descartes, having begun the third meditation with reference to the ideas in his mind that exist at least as his ideas, begins his argument by reviewing the sorts of ideas he has and their possible sources. He notes that some ideas 'seem to be born with me, others . . . to come from without, and the rest to be made . . . by myself' (Descartes 3, 36 [I, 160]). Again, in a letter to Mersenne written in 1641, the year the *Meditations* were published, Descartes draws this three-way distinction somewhat more technically: ideas may be '*adventitious*, such as the idea we . . . have of the sun; others are constructed or *factitious* [like] the idea which the astronomers have of the sun by their reasoning; and others are *innate*, such as the idea of God, [of] mind, body, triangle, and . . . eternal essences' (Kenny 1970, 104).

As he admits, chief among the possibilities regarding the origins of his ideas is that Descartes is himself their source, either conjuring them up, knowingly or unknowingly, or putting together a number of ideas to produce a single complex one – for instance, the idea of a unicorn as a compilation of the ideas of a horse and a golden horn. But it is crucial to Descartes' reflections on ideas and their possible sources that as effects of external causes or his own mind, ideas cannot be greater than their causes. He rearticulates the *ex nihilo* principle, saying that 'the light of nature' makes him recognize that 'ideas in me are like paintings or pictures,' and while they certainly can 'fall short of the perfection of the original from which they have been drawn,' ideas in his mind 'can never contain anything greater' (Descartes 3, 40 [I, 163]). Whether ideas' causes are internal or external, as effects they can never exceed their causes in any way.

The central notion here is initially plausible, being that if X produces Y, then Y initially cannot have more power or content than is found in X. Consider throwing a snowball. The thrown snowball can travel no further than the impetus received allows it to travel, nor can it impact on something with more force than that impetus and its mass jointly provide. Consider now rolling that same snowball down a steep, snowy hillside. By the time the snowball hits the base of the hill, it will have the mass it originally had plus the additional mass of snow picked up in rolling down the hill and whatever greater impetus it gained from gravity. When it hits, then, it will have a great deal more force than it started out with, and the effect it has may level a cabin. But we would not be tempted to say, except as a joke, that the cabin was leveled by a snowball, because we understand how the cause of the cabin's destruction was cumulative, how it was a small avalanche, not only the original snowball, and so the cause of the destruction of the cabin is equal to that effect. This is the sort of thinking Descartes is engaging in when he argues as he does, and we have no trouble understanding its direction or structure. The questions that arise have to do with how he characterizes the effect to which the argued-for cause must be adequate.

Descartes is arguing from a supposedly known effect – his idea of God – to an inaccessible cause – God. But it is a supposedly known effect because, as will emerge, the idea of God Descartes claims to have is problematic. Here we again see a shortfall in application of methodological doubt, in that Descartes does not consider seriously enough that his idea of God may be a composite one having several partly adequate causes. His rationale for rather quickly putting aside this possibility is that he has no convincing reason to think that his ideas, even when caused by external things, faithfully represent their causes.

Another shortfall in application of methodological doubt is that the evil-spirit hypothesis is unwarrantedly dismissed. Early in the third meditation Descartes tells us that he has no reason to believe that there is a deceiving God. What this amounts to is that the evil spirit ceases to be conceivable once the idea of a perfect – hence all-good and nondeceiving God enters the picture; and of course the idea of God in the third meditation must be of a perfect God because only then can it exceed Descartes' ability to concoct it out of his own imagination. The evil spirit is out of the picture the moment God is thought of as perfect; the evil-spirit hypothesis, then, is simply dropped once it serves its earlier purpose.

*   *   *

In describing his idea of God, Descartes provides us with a short list of God's major perfections, saying that by 'God' he means 'an infinite substance, independent, omniscient, omnipotent, and that by which I myself and all other existent things . . . have been created' (Descartes 3, 43 [I, 165]). What is crucial to the argument is that God's attributes are 'so great . . . that the more attentively I consider them, the less I can persuade myself that I could have derived them from my own nature,' so he must conclude that God exists (Descartes 3, 43 [I, 165]). Descartes concludes he could not himself be the source or cause of the idea of a perfect God, conveniently ignoring the possibility that the idea he has falls short of being of a perfect God and that its elements or components might be adventitious or factitious ideas as he himself defines them.

This point about the idea of God not quite being one of a perfect God is pivotal because to accept Descartes' argument, we must accept that we do have the idea of a perfect God. This is not to say we have to have a perfect idea of God, an idea which exhaustively captures God's essence; it is to say that it is at least not clear just what the idea of a perfect God is or entails. Consider a parallel: we have the idea that the series of natural numbers is an infinite series, so we have the idea of an infinite series. That sounds impressive until we realize that what we actually have is the idea that whatever number we come up with, we can always add one; we cannot conceive an infinite series in the sense of having a single, complete idea of one. The idea of an infinite series is, as we might put it, a performative one: what we have is not a single idea but understanding that we always can increase any natural number by one or more.

Descartes seems aware of our limitations with respect to the perfection of our ideas. In a 1642 letter to Regius, Descartes maintained that his causal argument for God's existence 'is based not on the essence of the idea, by which it is only a mode existing in the human mind and therefore no more perfect than a human being, but on its objective perfection' (Kenny 1970, 133). However, this is confusing. Recall that as he uses it, 'objective' here means the perfection of the idea of God as an object of awareness (See Chapter 1). If Descartes were referring to actual perfection, he would be referring to precisely what he is trying to establish, namely, a perfect God as the existent cause of the idea. What, then, is he distinguishing in separating the essence of the idea of God and the objective perfection of the idea of God? It seems all that this can come to is that the essence of the idea is what we can articulate about God, and of course we cannot capture God's perfection with a list of attributes such as omnipotence and omniscience. The objective perfection of the idea of God, then, has to be the nature or character of the idea as it is directly present to the mind. That perfection is not God's own perfection, since that cannot be caught in an idea. What Descartes must mean, therefore, is that the idea of God is present to the mind in a wholly compelling way, as an overwhelming given that allows no doubts about what it is. What Descartes no doubt thinks saves him from presupposing what he sets out to prove is that the objective perfection of the idea of God still leaves open the question about the actual reality or existence of God.

* * *

To recapitulate, any idea we entertain in our minds has a certain objective reality insofar as it is an object of consciousness: an idea 'is the thing thought of itself, in so far as it is objectively in the understanding' (Descartes, *Reply to Objections I*, Haldane and Ross 1969, Vol. II, 9). As an objective reality, in Descartes' sense, an idea requires either an internal or an external cause adequate to the idea as an effect. If the idea has an external cause, the actual reality of that cause must be at least as great as the idea's own objective reality. If the idea is internally caused, its objective reality is a function of the actual reality of the mind that entertains it. In the case of the idea of God, the idea's objective reality supposedly outstrips any degree of objective reality that Descartes' mind could bestow on it. The only thing that can be the adequate cause of the objective reality of the idea of God, the causal argument runs, is God's actual reality: only God's existence as perfect and infinite can be the cause of the objective reality of the idea of God.

Whatever its problems, Descartes' causal argument for the existence of God is his own, and that the argument is his own will emerge as significant when we consider the fifth meditation. At this juncture, though, more is to be gained by considering closely what the argument reveals about Descartes' conception of mind than pursuing the argument itself.

In offering a causal proof for the existence of God, Descartes reveals a good deal about how he conceives of the mind and its contents. Most significantly, those contents are taken as individual effects, thereby raising questions about their individual causes and their relations to those individual causes. In this regard, the idea of God and its allegedly perfect cause are simply a special instance of Descartes' conception of the mind's contents as effects – a conception that sets the scene for hundreds of years of epistemology by making it necessary to determine how faithful our ideas, as internal representational effects, are to their external causes.

What this conception of ideas as effects does is that it makes establishing as true ideas and beliefs based on them a matter of determining the independent reality of their causes and the ideas' representational accuracy with respect to their causes. As noted, trying to prove the existence of God by appealing to the necessary nature of the cause of the idea of God is only a special case of trying to demonstrate that our ideas are accurate, reliable representations of their causes, of things external to the mind. Achieving this is what Descartes makes the top priority for epistemology in particular and for modern philosophy in general. Our primary interest in the third meditation's causal argument for God's existence, then, is less in the hoary question of whether there is a God, than in the way Descartes tries to prove there is a God and in better understanding how Descartes thinks about ideas and their relation to the world.

* * *

As should now be clear, the most central points about how Descartes thinks about ideas is that ideas are internal to the mind; that each idea we entertain is potentially a representation of something, in being an effect of something; and that we human beings, as conscious, sentient creatures, of necessity face the epistemological task of determining which of our ideas represent realities and which do not. The trouble is, and this is to anticipate discussion of the sixth meditation, that the very conception of the mind as a container of possibly representational ideas ultimately precludes true knowledge of ideas' external causes.

As Hume's thought and work demonstrates, we cannot go beyond our ideas because, in the end, they cannot be independently shown to constitute knowledge of their putative causes. We cannot climb out of our minds to compare our ideas with their causes. We are left with our ideas – which Hume differentiates as impressions and ideas on the basis of vivacity – and with only conjectures about their possible causes (Audi 1996, 342–347; Honderich 1995, 377–381; Matson 2000, 411–437). Descartes' attempt to establish that at least one idea, the idea of God, somehow necessitates the reality of its independent cause, if it works, works only in the context of the presuppositions and assertions that the *Meditations* comprise.

Reference to the *Meditations'* presuppositions prompts attention to the charge of circularity often leveled against Descartes. The charge turns on a point alluded to the aforementioned, which has to do with the *ex nihilo* or adequate-cause principle and Descartes' espousal of it. The charge of circularity is that Descartes' causal argument for the existence of God relies on the *ex nihilo* principle, but that Descartes does not independently establish the principle in the *Meditations*, simply taking it as given that causes must be at least as great as their effects. It is important here that Descartes' espousal of the *ex nihilo* principle is not due merely to how the early Greeks and the Scholastics accepted the principle; Descartes treats the *ex nihilo* principle in the third meditation as a truth of reason. That he does so is evident from his description of the idea that causes must be adequate to their effects being something that he understands 'by the natural light [of reason]' (Cottingham 1995, 28).

The circularity then works in this way: The evil-spirit hypothesis has not been refuted, so it still is possible that the evil spirit is deceiving Descartes about truths of reason and about the adequate-cause principle in particular. But what would it take to refute the evil-spirit hypothesis? Descartes' *cogito* shows only that there are some things the evil spirit cannot deceive him about, but that does not of itself refute the evil-spirit hypothesis, so it remains possible that the evil spirit is still actively deceiving Descartes. The only thing that would establish that the evil spirit is not deceiving Descartes about the cause of the idea of God would be the idea being manifestly true as is the intuition of the *cogito*. But that it is would be difficult to make out and Descartes does not explicitly attempt to do so, though implicitly he does present the idea of God as having such a degree of objective reality that it is, in effect, indubitable.

As suggested earlier, what is necessary to refute the evil-spirit hypothesis is to establish that a perfect God exists, and that since a perfect God is an all-good and nondeceiving God, it is a God that would not tolerate the evil spirit deceiving Descartes, especially about anything as fundamental as God's own existence. It seems, then, that for the causal argument to work, Descartes needs the *ex nihilo* principle to be true, and since he is taking it as a truth of reason – one he cannot establish independently – Descartes needs to preclude that the evil spirit is deceiving him about the principle. But the only way to preclude that the evil spirit is deceiving him about the principle is to prove the existence of a perfect God, which is precisely what the causal argument is supposed to do, and for the argument to work Descartes needs the *ex nihilo* principle.

* * *

There is reason to feel, at the end of the third meditation, that the doubts raised in the first meditation have been too easily resolved in the second and especially in the third – and this is quite aside from how methodological doubt is not consistently applied at various points in the second and third meditations. As we shall see when we consider the argument for God's existence offered in the fifth meditation and particularly the attempt to prove the existence of matter in the sixth meditation, Descartes does not again offer anything as compelling as the proof of his own existence. If we waive the problem of Descartes too quickly moving from his thinking to his being a thinking thing, his intuition about his own existence begins to look less like a discerned sample of self-evident truth than like the only evident truth Descartes discerns.

The third meditation makes abundantly clear that Descartes manifests greater confidence in his critical ability than he has reason to, given the effectiveness of the dream and evil-spirit hypotheses. He tells us that the more he examines the various points he makes in the meditation, the more clearly and distinctly he recognizes their truth (Cottingham 1995, 29).

If one is being charitable, it is arguable that Descartes has some reason to feel confident, given the force of the *cogito*. That is, it can be argued that his intuition that he exists as he thinks is forceful enough to reassure him about his own discriminatory powers and not so much to defeat the dream and evil-spirit hypotheses as to make them look faintly ridiculous. Descartes himself takes up something of this practical approach in the third meditation when he emphasizes the differences among ideas in terms of their vivacity, force, detail, and mode of presentation, something noticeably absent in the first two meditations and which certainly makes at least the dream hypothesis less persuasive (Cottingham 1995, 25–26). But this confidence that Descartes may be justified in feeling is not philosophically grounded. It is, as just said, a matter of being practical and amounts only to realizing that once the *cogito* has done its work, the overly scrupulous skepticism of methodological doubt begins to look uncalled for and artificial. The conclusion one is prompted to draw is that the *Meditations* fail as philosophy in general and epistemology in particular, though they succeed in casting doubt on the point and value of doing epistemology and philosophy as Descartes sets out to do them. But there are three more meditations to consider; we must reserve judgment, though we must keep in mind the several ways that

Descartes contentions and arguments fall short of the standards he himself sets in the first meditation.

* * *

What we are left with at the end of the third meditation are a sample of indubitable truth, certainty about our own existence, understanding of what defines possibly existent material objects, all from the second meditation, and an all-good, nondeceiving God from the third. Descartes contends that all four items are the products of methodological doubt applied to ideas and beliefs we already had, analysis of those beliefs and ideas, and discernment of clear and distinct truth by the natural light of reason. What is gained is that we now purportedly have indubitably true ideas and beliefs whereas before we had ones we only accepted as true. We now know we exist whereas before we just did not question that we do; now we comprehend what makes material objects material, if they exist, whereas before we took them for granted; and now we know there is a God whereas before we only believed in God. If Descartes decided to stop at the end of the third meditation, his contribution to philosophy would have been momentous. And as we shall see in the chapters that follow, perhaps Descartes would have been well advised to stop at the end of the third meditation.

Considering the relative brevity of the first three meditations, it is nothing short of amazing what their contents supposedly establish. But the implications of what Descartes thinks he achieves are even more amazing. For one thing, if Descartes is right, relativistic philosophies, and especially contemporary postmodernism, are radically confused or just wrong in eschewing absolute truth and making truth historical and perspectival. For another, atheism and all forms of polytheism also are radically confused or just wrong because God does exist and, being perfect, must be singular.

If Descartes is right about what he establishes by the end of the third meditation, the *Meditations*, which have been available for some three-hundred-and-sixty years, are without doubt the world's most important philosophical work. Moreover, philosophy since 1641 should be nothing more than development of Descartes' position, as Whitehead claimed that all philosophy was so many footnotes to Plato. Yet Descartes' position is now seen by many as important only in a historical sense and is rejected by at least as many. Clearly there are relatively few who think Descartes is right, but before we draw our own conclusions, we have three more meditations to consider.

SUMMARY

Summarizing the third meditation is a little tricky and requires more extensive discussion that a summary should involve. However, there are good reasons for this. One is that the third meditation's main argument is clear enough as presented and as considered earlier, but the problem posed is less the argument than what we are to make of the argument: how we are to understand it and in particular its premise about objective reality. What follows, then, is less a summary than it is a reiteration and slight expansion of the key points.

As much of the present chapter should make clear, the third meditation is in some ways more important because of the material surrounding the causal argument for God's existence than because of the argument itself. What Descartes does in the third meditation that is as important as the causal argument he offers is to distinguish the kinds of ideas that make up the contents of his mind. He distinguishes among ideas that are innate in him; ideas that come or seem to come from causes external to his mind; and ideas that he conjures up himself. Of these, the sort that concerns him in the third meditation are ideas that come or seem to come from causes external to his mind, and one of those ideas, his particular interest, is the idea of God.

This is where things get complicated. The idea of God, Descartes contends, does not only seem to have an external cause, as do ideas that present themselves as of objects in the world. The basis of his causal argument is that the objective reality of the idea of God is so great that the idea is presented to the mind in a way that makes the externality of its cause somehow undeniable. The most generous way of taking this contention is to understand it as the idea of God being such that it is obvious to those having it present to their minds that they could not have produced it themselves. There is a sense, then, in which the causal argument is less an argument than it is a kind of clarification, an articulation of an intuition that is not unlike the intuition that is the essence of the *cogito*. Differently put, articulation of the causal argument has as its point less demonstrating the truth of God's existence than enabling people to appreciate fully what they already know but have not recognized or acknowledged. This is how the causal argument is similar to the articulation of the intuition of the *cogito*.

Only an existent perfect God could be the cause or source of the idea of God. Reliance on the *ex nihilo* principle, the principle that an effect's cause must have as much reality or potency as the effect manifests, is reliance on a truth of reason and suffices to make the point. However, all of this turns on acceptance of Descartes' claim that the idea of God has a unique and overwhelming measure of objective reality, and what remains unclear is just what that is.

Perhaps the best way to end this summary, and to restate the basic problem with Descartes' causal argument, is to quote the criticism raised by one of his own contemporaries. The criticism centers on three points: first, that Descartes claims 'that there is in the idea of an infinite God more objective reality than in the idea of a finite thing'; second, that Descartes uses that measure of objective reality to argue that only a perfect God could be its cause; but third, the contention that 'the human intellect is not capable of conceiving of infinity, and hence it neither has nor can contemplate any idea representing an infinite thing' (Cottingham 1995, 81).

Descartes offers a lengthy reply to the criticism, but adds little to what he says in the third meditation itself. He would do better to maintain – as is the case – that he is not claiming that we do have an idea representing an infinite thing, but rather that the idea we do have, however short it may fall of being of an infinite thing, nonetheless is possessed of a compelling measure of objective reality. However, that only brings us back to our own question: just what is it for an idea to have such objective reality?

The trouble is that there is no convincing answer to this question. Descartes is claiming that the idea of God, though not itself perfect, nonetheless has a degree of objective reality – and remember this refers to its reality as an object of thought – that cannot be explained by or attributed to anything other than a perfect cause. But what is it for an idea to have that degree of objective reality?

Notice that we cannot say, as some no doubt would say, that the idea presents itself as indubitably true, as does the intuition of the *cogito*. The reason we cannot say this is that the intuition of the *cogito* is of or about Descartes own existence whereas with the idea of God the issue of truth is about the idea's cause, not the idea itself. Differently put, what the intuition of the *cogito* establishes as true is given in the thinking or articulating of the *cogito* or the 'I think, I am,' but the cause of the idea of God cannot be given in the idea of God. That would eradicate the difference between the objective reality of the idea of God and God's own actual reality. And if Descartes succumbs to saying that what he means by the special objective reality of the idea of God is that the idea somehow incorporates verification of the actual reality of its own cause, the causal argument becomes redundant because the idea of God simply is cast as self-verifying as the *cogito* intuition is self-verifying.

In the final analysis, Descartes' claim about the idea of God having a compelling measure of objective reality fails to bear the weight he needs to bear. If nothing else, the thought persists that so long as the idea is not itself perfect, it is possible that its claimed objective reality is the result of cumulative, composite causes rather than of a single divine cause. It is precisely that Descartes' argument is a causal one, and hence an *a posteriori* or one dependent on experience, that keeps the cumulative-cause explanation viable (See Glossary). In other words, so long as the argument is causal and not purely conceptual, there is no way to conclusively rule out alternative causal explanations. When we consider Descartes' version of the Ontological argument for God's existence, in the fifth meditation, it will emerge that Descartes' purported causal argument in fact may not be a causal or *a posteriori* argument, but actually be only another version of the *a priori* Ontological argument. The original Ontological argument was formulated by the medieval philosopher and theologian Anselm of Canterbury (1033–1109) and is called 'ontological' because it purports to establish the existence of something – God – on the basis of an understanding of its nature.

Arguments regarding God's existence long preceded Descartes' efforts and continue to be offered (Matson 1965). But their success seems to be a direct function of prior faith rather than of logic or marshaling of evidence. Descartes' third-meditation argument is novel, and has prompted much discussion, but in the end, what is more philosophically important in the third meditation is what Descartes says about ideas. His classification of ideas as adventitious, innate, or products of his own mind has huge implications for epistemology and especially the empiricism that followed. The key point is less the distinctions than their exhaustiveness because the three-way classification of the contents of our minds severs our connection to the world by making it one mediated by ideas. Adventitious ideas, the ideas we have that seem to be of things external to our mind, are the closest we get to the things themselves; we have no direct access to anything beyond the contents of our own minds. The reality of the causes of adventitious ideas has to be established argumentatively. The consequence is that Descartes isolates consciousness from everything that is not consciousness. Foucault sums up this isolation of consciousness in a beautifully tight observation: 'Hume has become possible' (Foucault 1973, 60).

Descartes makes it possible to think that the contents of our mind are all we can know and might be all that there is because ultimately the external causes of ideas must forever remain conjectural, however strongly supported by argument and experience. Descartes thus set epistemology, the theory of knowledge, on a hopeless more than 300-year search for conclusive evidence that something exists outside the mind – including other minds.

Some readers may well feel that this so-called summary of the present chapter should itself be summarized, but while reiteration is necessary to get straight on Descartes' claims, it should not be too obviously overdone. In any case the next chapter offers a recapitulation of the most important points made in the first three meditations, again with a view to ensuring clarity.

CHAPTER 6

A BRIEF INTERLUDE

Before moving on to the fourth of Descartes' meditations, we need to take stock of a number of points raised by the first three. The main reason there is need to take stock is that the first and second meditations provide what is most novel and persuasive in Descartes' thought, and the third, though it centers on a less than persuasive argument for God's existence, does offer some original thought in the formulation of the argument offered and contains some of the most epistemologically consequential implications of any of the six meditations. Against this, the fourth, fifth, and sixth meditations are of considerably less philosophical importance: the fourth offers a clever but essentially extraneous argument and the fifth offers little more than a truncated version of Anselm's Ontological argument. As for the sixth meditation, the long delayed 'proof' of the existence of extended matter marks something of a low point in cogency. It will prove productive, then, to recapitulate what is most import- ant in the first three meditations, and hence in the whole of the *Meditations on First Philosophy*, and to do so in terms that make clear the essential points and contentions we find in Descartes' best known and most widely read work.

*   *   *

We need to begin with methodological doubt. Whether articulated and employed in terms of the dream and evil-spirit hypotheses or with other devices, the heart of Descartes' notion is that it is too difficult and unreliable to proceed by raising epistemological questions about individual problematic matters. The best thing to do, if one is serious about the quest for truth, is not to doubt beliefs and potential beliefs in a piecemeal way, but to level all beliefs by not just doubting them, but by actually assuming them to be false until they are demonstrated to be true. Descartes tells us that he will pretend, 'for a time,' that everything he accepts or believes, all the things he takes as given or true, 'are utterly false and imaginary' (Cottingham 1995, 15). This is what the dream and evil-spirit hypotheses serve to do: they provide reasons for willfully taking everything believed to be false unless and until what is believed is seen to be indubitably true by the natural light of reason.

Descartes' heroic skeptical efforts, however, almost immediately show themselves to be inadvertently selective, granting that he is not knowingly picking and choosing what to doubt and what not to doubt. The most salient shortfall in application of methodological doubt is Descartes' failure to apply it to the idea of substance and to the *ex nihilo* principle, both of which he takes as given. But at least as serious a failure is how Descartes limits his skepticism to the objects of thought and does not apply it to the process of thought itself.

In applying methodological doubt to the objects of thought, Descartes distinguishes early in the third meditation among the contents of his mind with respect to what is capable of being true or false. In doing so, he reminds us that there is more in the mind than ideas of things, but here we encounter an ambiguity that threatens to vitiate much of what he contends (Cottingham 1995, 24–26). At times Descartes speaks as if all the mind contains are ideas, and at other times he speaks as if there is more, like when he acknowledges that the mind also contains volitions or acts of will, emotions, and judgments.

The likeliest interpretation is that Descartes sometimes uses 'ideas' in an inclusive sense, and sometimes in a narrower, exclusive sense. In any case, judgments enter the picture when, in reviewing his progress at the opening of meditation three, Descartes considers the kinds of thoughts he has and which 'can be properly said to be the bearers of truth and falsity' (Cottingham 1995, 25). Recall consideration in Chapter 3 about how ideas might be true in themselves or be presented to the mind as true in themselves. The essential point there was that from our own perspective, what are true or false are propositions or statements or beliefs. But Descartes, apparently relegating language to a subordinate position, ascribes truth to ideas themselves.

What emerges more clearly in the third meditation in Descartes' acknowledgment of judgments is that though he sometimes does sound as if it is ideas themselves that are true, in at least some cases when considering what it is that is true Descartes holds that it is judgments that are true or false. This is evident when he tells us that ideas, 'considered solely in themselves' and not referred to their possible causes, 'cannot strictly speaking be false; for whether it is a goat or a chimera that I am imagining, it is just as true that I imagine the former as the latter' (Cottingham 1995, 26). In other words, ideas as bare presentations to the mind are neutral with respect to truth or falsity because, in themselves, they simply are objects of thought in the minimal sense of being objects given to awareness.

Notice that Descartes' comment does not quite say that ideas cannot present themselves as true, that is, that they are or may be apprehended as true without exercise of judgment, but the remark does make it sound as if references to ideas presenting themselves as true is a form of shorthand in which reference to judgment is implicit rather than explicit. The likelihood, then, seems to be that what are true or false are judgments, for instance the judgment that the idea of a goat is true – or, more carefully put, the judgment that the idea's objective reality accurately represents its cause, a goat as an actually existent thing.

In all of this, Descartes construes judgment in a very limited manner. It is hard to decide whether it is his limited construal of judgment that facilitates Descartes' thinking of some ideas as presenting themselves as indubitably true, or whether it is thinking of ideas as so presenting themselves that narrows construal of judgment. In any case, as Descartes presents it, judgment is assenting or not assenting to presented ideas, as if judgment consisted of nodding 'yes' or shaking the head 'no' when shown a picture and being asked if one likes it or not.

We of course cannot hold Descartes responsible for not anticipating Kant and considering the role of conceptualization in the shaping and the making of judgments about the contents of consciousness. That is, we cannot fault Descartes for not factoring in to his thinking about judging ideas true or false the fact that nothing is just given to the mind: that everything which is an object of awareness is defined as such by our concepts, and that judgments about everything that is an object of awareness always are judgments about what we conceptualize in one or another way. Descartes' lack of understanding of the role of conceptualization perhaps is clearest in his causal argument for the existence of God, because the purported objective reality of the idea of a perfect God is due to how Descartes conceives of God, not to an idea's intrinsic properties.

In general, the Kantian point is that nothing presents itself to awareness in a determinate manner, whether it is a product of an external cause or of the mind itself. Everything of which we are conscious, every object of thought is shaped by our concepts, and the importance of conceptualization's role in the present context has to do with how significant to Descartes' thinking is reliance on visual metaphors. It is that reliance that casts ideas as wholly determinate products of external causes or internal processes, and it is this determinacy which underlies and to a large extent enables Descartes' contentions about the clarity and distinctness of some idea. This is because determinacy is a prerequisite of ideas being clear and distinct and therefore being recognized as indubitably true by the natural light.

Once ideas are determinate in this way, judgment can be portrayed as assent to ideas or rejection of them, as when an idea of a horse is assented to as accurately representing its cause, the horse in the external world, and an idea of a unicorn is rejected as false and only a product of the mind as either a composite idea or an illusory one.

* * *

It is difficult to avoid drawing two negative conclusions regarding Descartes' methodological doubt. The first conclusion is straightforward: Descartes simply fails to apply methodological doubt as rigorously as he sets out to do. As noted, the most evident failures to apply methodological doubt rigorously are that Descartes does not question either of two key philosophical notions he uses; he uses both without assessing each as we expect him to, given what we are told in the first meditation about doubting everything. One notion is the early Greek *ex nihilo* or adequate-cause principle; the other notion is the Aristotelian and Scholastic doctrine of substances and their defining properties. Were Descartes applying methodological doubt rigorously, he would not avail himself of either of these notions without critically examining each, but instead of doing so he accepts them as evident truths of reason.

The less straightforward negative conclusion also is about failure to apply methodological doubt, but because of certain presuppositions and implications the failure is more complicated than Descartes simply not critically examining two philosophical notions he employs.

There are two parts to the complicated failure; one is that Descartes never questions the reliability of his own memory as he pursues his arguments. Someone claiming to be applying methodological doubt rigorously should consider if memory can be relied upon regarding such things as moving from one premise to another when framing an argument. If the evil spirit is capable of deceiving Descartes about five and five making ten, it is capable of deceiving him about his arguments by making him forget a premise as he proceeds to the next or draws a conclusion. The trouble is that it is not clear how Descartes could get beyond the first meditation if he did doubt his own memory. Here again we see why many have argued that all that actually is demonstrated in the *Meditations* is that thought is taking place when the *cogito* is articulated.

The second part of the complicated failure is that as with memory, Descartes does not question the reliability of language in his reflections. This is a failure that like the one regarding Descartes' naïveté about conceptualization, seems unfair to press because to do so would be anachronistic. Nonetheless, it does not seem too much to expect Descartes to wonder if his use of various terms like 'idea' is consistent throughout his meditations or if ambiguities creep in over the span of the six meditations.

It is important to note before proceeding that readers new to philosophy may feel that the foregoing and much in previous chapters is too critical of a work that is described as pivotal in philosophy. This feeling is a likely response in our time, when criticism is seen as 'offensive' and people are concerned not to be 'judgmental.' But this response misses the point of philosophical thinking, the essence of which precisely is critical assessment. The aim of criticism throughout this book is not denigration of Descartes' claims and contentions but achievement of better understanding of those claims and contentions, and a crucial element in achievement of such understanding is getting clear on where his arguments go wrong. With respect to the *Meditations* in particular and philosophizing in general, it is not too much to say that a reluctance to critically assess claims and contentions is preclusive of learning and certainly of doing philosophy well.

* * *

The *cogito* is, of course, absolutely central to the *Meditations*, and at first sight it may look invulnerable to criticism. But here, too, there are problems. The outstanding one, considered in Chapter 4, has to do with Descartes' concluding that he is a thinking thing, a mental substance, from his intuition that in thinking he manifests his existence. Strictly speaking, all that the *cogito* intuition establishes is that thought exists, that thinking is taking place, at the time that the intuition is grasped or articulated.

It may seem acceptable to assume self-reference to oneself as a thinker in the *cogito* intuition; that is, it appears unproblematic to take the intuition as Descartes does, as establishing beyond question that he and each of us exists as he or we engage in thought. But questions do arise about self-identity because as Descartes formulates and uses the *cogito* – 'I think, I am' – the 'I' clearly refers to more than the immediate thought, which strictly speaking is all that 'I' should refer to. The *cogito* could be reformulated as 'A thought is taking place' and nothing would be lost regarding demonstration of existence at that moment. In other words, the question about self-identity is about how much is packed into the 'I' in 'I think, I am,' and this question immediately raises the further question about the move from thinking to a thinking thing, a substance.

The only sanction Descartes has for the move from the 'I' of the *cogito* to an existent substance of which the thought is a property is his conviction that thinking is, indeed, a property, and hence cannot exist on its own. Descartes takes it as given that establishing that thinking is taking place establishes that something exists that is doing that thinking. As has been pointed out, Descartes does not argue for this point; he simply asserts it because he never questions the conception of substances and their properties that he inherits from Aristotle through the Scholastics. Descartes cannot conceive that thought might be occurring and be all there is, as Hume managed to conceive.

Both the questions about self-identity and about the too-ready move to an existent thinking substance pose another problem with the *cogito*, alluded to earlier, which is that Descartes takes the evidence of the *cogito* intuition as establishing not only that the 'I' in the 'I think, I am' refers to himself as a thinking thing, but that he remains the same thinking thing, thought after thought, over a substantial period of time – at least as long as it takes him to think through the second meditation. Here again we see the depth of Descartes' commitment to the substance doctrine, for he obviously is thinking that once he establishes himself as a thinking thing, his continuation as that thinking thing is not something that needs to be demonstrated.

What we must conclude regarding the *cogito* intuition is that while the essential point that thinking demonstrates existence is unchallengeable, the point yields only that existence is demonstrated while thought is taking place. The intuition does not establish the existence, self-identity, and continuity of a thinking thing. Here we must side with Hume and accept that while the existence of thought cannot be doubted while it is taking place, nothing follows from that about whether there is a thinker distinct from the thought that is taking place.

*   *   *

We come now to the causal argument for God's existence. Enough has been said about Descartes' problematic and unreflective acceptance of the *ex nihilo* or adequate-cause principle, without which his causal argument cannot work. But there is another issue that needs to be mentioned. It is crucial to Descartes' argument that the idea of God from which he argues is the idea of a perfect God. The alternatives are numerous: for instance, there might be more than one God; God might be limited in time; God might not be omnipotent; God might not be omniscient; God might not be all-good and tolerate evil. It is only if Descartes begins with the idea of a perfect God that he can argue as he does that the cause of the idea can only be a perfect God.

As we saw earlier, one criticism leveled against Descartes' causal argument is that we are incapable of having an idea of a perfect or infinite God. But aside from whether or not we can grasp perfection or at least enough of it to proceed with Descartes' causal argument, consider other questions that arise about God's putative perfections. For example, along with omnipotence and omniscience, the trait or perfection most often attributed to a perfect God is unlimited goodness. God usually is characterized as all-powerful, all-knowing, and all-good.

A perfect God being all-good entails that God is merciful, since mercy is a constituent of goodness or at least is invariably so presented. It is hardly surprising that human beings, cast by their clergies as sinners and seeing themselves as sinners, are concerned about God's mercifulness, but there is no question that for whatever reasons, a perfect God is understood as being merciful. Moreover, any attribute possessed by a perfect God is possessed in perfect measure. This is where problems start, because if God is perfect, then another of God's attributes is being just, and given that God is perfect, being just also is an attribute possessed in perfect measure. The difficulty, then, is that mercy precisely is a tempering of justice for particular reasons in particular circumstances. The question, therefore, is how perfect justice can be tempered to accommodate perfect mercifulness. When exercised, mercy and justice qualify one another, but if each is perfectly exercised, there seems no possibility of tempering justice in order to show mercy.

Another worrying question is posed by the philosophical and theological distinction drawn between *a priori* and *a posteriori* arguments for God's existence – a distinction between arguments that appeal to reason alone and arguments that appeal to reason and experience. This distinction is of major significance regarding the difference between Descartes' causal or *a posteriori* argument for God's existence in the third meditation, and Descartes' version of Anselm's Ontological or *a priori* argument in the fifth meditation. The problem here has to do with how Descartes' *a posteriori* causal argument tends to collapse into an *a priori* argument because of the emphasis put on the idea of God as perfect.

Aquinas provides a useful contrast because of the care he took to avoid offering any version of the Ontological argument, due to his reservations about Anselm's argument seeming to require a degree of knowledge about God's nature that Aquinas thought human beings could not achieve and which it was theologically risky for them to claim they had achieved. Aquinas offered no fewer than five *a posteriori* arguments for God's existence, with a view to demonstrating the reality of an entity having each of five key attributes and only then arguing that the five attributes were possessed by the same entity, namely, God.

In each of the arguments Aquinas draws his conclusion about the entity each argument purports to show exists – for instance, one argument establishes the existence of a 'First Cause' of all that exists (Matson 1965). Only when the argument is done does Aquinas say that the First Cause is God. The reason Aquinas proceeds as he does is that none of the individual five arguments he offers presupposes knowledge or understanding not made available to reason in each of the arguments.

Unlike Aquinas, Descartes' causal argument, which is – supposedly – an *a posteriori* argument because it is based on experience of the idea of a perfect God, assumes that we do have the idea of a perfect God. All Descartes offers in support of this assumption is a list of attributes that we supposedly recognize as elements of the idea of a perfect God. But each attribute can be argued against, as in the case of perfect mercy, or might be rejected for theological reasons, depending on the theology endorsed. For instance, God may be conceived as in process and hence not infinite in time or only approaching omniscience. All of this is precisely why Descartes' contemporaries argued against him that he was presupposing an ability to grasp perfection, because it is only if we do grasp perfection, in the sense of having at least an adequate idea of God's perfection, of a perfect God, that we can accept Descartes' claim that the cause of that idea can only be an existent perfect God.

The point here is not to initiate complex theological discussions; it is only to show that as with self-identity and substance, Descartes again lets a serious issue slip by that methodological doubt decidedly should not let slip by. We cannot expect Descartes to review the bulk of theology regarding conception of God as perfect, but we can expect him to examine the idea of a perfect God more thoroughly than he does. What he offers in the third meditation is not analysis of the idea of a perfect God but an inventory of the attributes the idea carries with it but which are, in fact, arguable. The result is that the claimed objective reality of the idea does not support his claim that its only possible cause is an actually existent perfect God. Additionally, as will emerge when we consider his version of the Ontological argument, Descartes' treatment of the idea of a perfect God approaches turning thought of God's perfection from an *a posteriori* consequence of experience of the idea of a perfect God, as it should be for the argument to be a causal one, to an *a priori* thought. To the extent that this happens, the causal argument of the third meditation collapses into the Ontological argument of the fifth meditation.

* * *

My aim in this chapter is not to disconcert you about Descartes' arguments by piling up criticisms, or to undermine the importance of the *Meditations*; it is to provide you with the most thorough understanding of Descartes' work that can be made available in an introductory text. Assuming that this recapitulation has advanced that intention, we can now proceed to consider Descartes' fourth meditation.

CHAPTER 7

THE FOURTH MEDITATION: EXPLAINING THE POSSIBILITY OF ERROR

Our considerations of each of the fourth, fifth, and sixth meditations will be more concise than those of the first three. While important issues are raised in the fourth, fifth, and sixth meditations, and Descartes makes significant contentions in them, you will see that their content is of lesser philosophical consequence than are the introduction of methodological doubt in the first meditation, articulation of the *cogito* in the second, and Descartes' causal argument for God's existence in the third. Treatment of error in the fourth meditation is mainly done for theological reasons; presentation of a version of the Ontological argument in the fifth meditation offers little that is new to supplement Anselm's original formulation of the argument; and the purported demonstration of the existence of extended matter in the sixth meditation is decidedly anticlimactic.

The aim of the fourth meditation is to deal with a problem that arises for Descartes because of his conception of God as perfect and hence as all-good. The problem is how to explain why a perfect, all-good God allows error. Though there is no explicit reference to what is usually called 'the problem of evil' – how a perfect God tolerates evil and allows people to damn themselves – it is obvious that it is the problem of evil Descartes addresses, though he does so in restricted terms of error in judgment.

The most common way of dealing with the problem of evil is to argue that God allows it because human beings were created with free will to bear responsibility for their choices and actions, and that unfortunately they often choose to do wrong (Matson 1965, 135–170). But without free will, and so without the possibility of willingly doing wrong, people could not earn salvation by their righteous choices, good works, and willful avoidance of wrongdoing. If human beings are to be moral agents, they must have free will even if it is at the cost of allowing evil and self-damnation. Though he adds an ingenious element, Descartes' proposed resolution of the problem posed by error is very similar to the traditional free-will response to the problem of evil in that he makes us, as beings possessed of free will, responsible for error.

* * *

Descartes structures his treatment of why error occurs and is tolerated by God in a basically epistemological way. His doing so is prompted by his employment of error to generate skepticism about sensory perception in developing methodological doubt. As Descartes understands it, we make mistakes in judging or 'assenting to' ideas as representations of external reality when the ideas either are not representations of anything or are representations but are distorted or false in some way. But not only do we make mistakes in wrongly assenting to some ideas as representations when they are not or are inaccurate representations, Descartes further describes perception as systematically deceptive because aside from particular errors, sensory perception presents some properties – notably colors – as if they are properties of the things in the world themselves, when the properties actually are caused in us by other properties of the things themselves, such as surface-texture.

It would appear, therefore, that both the errors we make in assenting to nonrepresentational or distorted ideas, and in taking properties like colors to be in the things themselves, ultimately are not our fault but are God's fault for not giving us better intellectual and sensory abilities. This possibility is theologically worrying because it implies one of two equally unacceptable possibilities: either God intended to create us better but could not do so because of limited power, which entails that God is not omnipotent and thus not perfect; or God is omnipotent but deliberately created us less well than possible, which entails that God is not all-good and thus, again, not perfect.

Having made as much of error as he does in developing method-ological doubt, Descartes is obliged to explain the possibility of error in order not to impugn either God's omnipotence or infinite goodness. Descartes cannot let his arguments in the first three meditations imply that God is somehow responsible for our mistakes; he must explain error in a way that does not impugn either God's power or benevolence. However, Descartes cannot undo his epistemological strategy by rescinding his reliance on the undeniable fact that we err as individuals and on his observation that properties which visual perception systematically leads us to believe are properties of external objects actually are properties of our internal ideas.

In connection with this last point, a brief clarification is called for because some readers might be puzzled as to how the perceptually systematic projection of colors – taking color as the simplest example – onto the things themselves counts as error on our part. The Cartesian answer is simple: we need to take greater care in judging the actual location of sensory properties; that is what the doing of science is all about. We need to investigate and analyze not only every idea, but every kind of idea to understand the precise nature of what ideas individually and as types represent – when they do, in fact, represent something.

Descartes' solution is to argue that God is not at fault regarding error because God gave us all the intellectual ability and accuracy of perception we need. If we err, it is our fault for not using our abilities properly. The way Descartes makes out his contention that it is we who are to blame for error begins with his recalling that since we must be free to choose between good and evil to be moral agents, God had to give us perfectly free wills. Descartes reminds us that a will's freedom cannot be qualified; a will either is free or it is not free. Despite being omnipotent, God had no choice but to give each of us a perfectly free will because if our wills were restricted in some way regarding our choices and decisions, we could not be held morally responsible for some or all of our actions.

Contemporary beliefs and attitudes necessitate another brief clarification at this point because many present-day readers may not fully appreciate the point about responsibility – a point that would have been integral to Descartes' thinking. The historical fact is that we now know too much about psychology to think that people's choices and actions ever are entirely free, and we no longer hold people responsible for their actions to the degree Descartes took for granted. Moreover, the historical drift seems clearly to be toward reducing further the degree to which we hold people responsible for their actions. We now find ourselves in a social context where behavioral 'syndromes' are rife and new ones seem to be discovered daily; what people do is being increasingly 'medicalized' in that their actions are more and more being attributed to various influences on them throughout their personal histories, rather than being deemed to be the results of their own independent choices.

The inclination toward reducing responsibility for behavior is not limited to our social interactions and legal systems. If we compare present-day interpretations of secular norms and religious doctrines regarding moral conduct with the interpretations of Descartes' age we find a marked softening in the degree to which contemporaries are held responsible for their moral actions. As you read the fourth meditation and the rest of this chapter, therefore, you have to keep in mind that Descartes is working with a conception of agent-responsibility in which individuals earn their places in heaven or eternal damnation entirely on their own merits: that is, on the basis of choices deemed to be wholly their own. This is why Descartes saw moral responsibility as requiring a perfect will. For him, human beings have to be capable of totally free choices to act morally or immorally, and for them to do so – and given what is at stake in their doing so – their wills must be totally free and their actions held to be entirely the products of their own decisions.

* * *

Given that Descartes' causal argument is supposed to establish the existence of a perfect, omnipotent, omniscient, all-good God, and God created us with free will, what is Descartes' next step? His next essential point is that God was under no obligation from beneficence to create us with perfect intellects. God created us with intellects adequate to cope with our lives and world and, we must remember, adequate to establishing God's existence as well as our own existence. Despite the adequacy of our intellects, though, when we reason and draw conclusions or assent to ideas presented to us in perception, we sometimes get things wrong. The trick now is to show that our sometimes getting things wrong is not a direct function of our having been given only adequate intellects, else our errors would be God's fault, even if only indirectly.

The ingenious part of Descartes' argument is his contention that the reason we sometimes get things wrong is that our perfect wills unduly override our merely adequate intellects in the sense that we judge hastily. Descartes argues that error arises from the interaction of our intellect and our free will, but in a way that is not due to our intellects being only adequate, and therefore error arises in a way that is not attributable to God because of how we were created.

The way Descartes' solution works is as follows: the intellect neither affirms ideas as true nor rejects them as false by itself. When ideas are presented to the mind, most call for judgments to be made regarding their representational nature or status, but the judgments need to be made as acts of the will. Judgments are, after all, acts, and as such they require volition to be performed. Error arises because our free wills prompt hasty judgments: precipitous assent or rejection of ideas on deficient bases. Additionally, the will sometimes prompts assent or rejection of ideas that we do not even understand (Descartes 4, 54, 56 [I, 175, 176]). Error, then, is due to rash judgments prompted by our unlimited wills.

The question arises why our wills prompt hasty judgments. Is it some flaw in our wills that causes error? Does God still bear responsibility for error for creating us with the wills we have? No, not at all. What needs to be understood is that it is not the will itself that prompts hasty judgments. It is we who exercise our wills, who judge rashly, because we are driven by our interests and desires. We go wrong when what we expect or want or fear causes us to fail to analyze and assess carefully the ideas presented to the mind and so to impetuously draw unwarranted conclusions. The will, like the intellect, is an instrument. The trouble is that there are things we want to be the case or not be the case because of what we desire or think is in our interests. We then judge some things to be as we would prefer them to be or fear they might be instead of observing carefully just how they actually are. The fault for error is ours, not our Creator's.

Descartes' attribution of error to hasty judgment is supposed to make clear to us that once we grasp the cause of error in judgment, we will more fully appreciate the necessity of using the analytic procedures developed in application of methodological doubt. We will better understand that the way to cope with our limited intellects is to be rigorous in our assessment of what calls for judgment. In this way, the resolution of the problem posed by error reinforces the call for critical analysis and productive skepticism. Descartes believes that if we proceed in the making of judgments with appropriate care, our limited intellects will serve us competently, as our Creator intended they should. Moreover, that they can serve us competently is evident in Descartes' own successful demonstrations of his own existence and of the existence of God.

The result, then, is that we are to blame for error, not God: we misuse our admittedly limited intellects by allowing our free wills to rush us into making ill-informed decisions, drawing unmerited conclusions, and generally giving or withholding our assent to ideas injudiciously or lacking sufficient understanding. If we are careful, if we apply productive skepticism and thorough analysis, and if we draw conclusions only when they can be soundly drawn, we will not err and our limited intellects will be shown to be wholly adequate to our needs.

Consider now some responses to Descartes' account of error as due to our free wills improperly overriding our limited intellects, as well as Descartes' likely rejoinders. We might point out to Descartes that a perfect and truly benevolent God would have anticipated the results of harnessing a perfect will to an imperfect intellect and have arranged a better balance between the will and intellect in creating us. If there could be no restriction of the will, our intellects could have been made better or our impulsive inclinations tempered. Descartes' rejoinder no doubt would be to maintain that the possibility of error due to the will overriding the intellect was the price to be paid for our being free and hence capable of being moral agents, and that the only possible better arrangement would have been for God to give us perfect intellects and so make us virtual gods.

If we ask what would be so wrong with our having perfect intellects, the rejoinder almost certainly would be that by making us virtual gods, God would be depriving us of the opportunity to earn our salvation and entry into heaven. Our equally obvious response to this rejoinder is that a truly benevolent God would have created us as heavenly residents in the first place and simply bypassed our inevitably arduous Earthly existence. The likeliest rejoinder to this would be to eulogize the value of meriting salvation as a 'second order' good – that is, as a good possible and attainable only through the triumph over evil. As in arguments about the problem of evil, the inevitable response here would be that so-called second order goods are *ad hoc* and only necessary to justify why a supposedly perfect and all-good God allows error or evil.

In any case, whatever we may think of Descartes' explanation of error, he does manage to avoid a theologically dangerous situation in which his reliance on error to substantiate the skepticism of methodological doubt might be read by some as indirectly attributing blame to God for our mistakes.

* * *

Despite the ingenuity of Descartes' solution to the error issue, the solution raises questions because of what it implies about his conception of the mind – questions that eventually may prove more serious to the cogency of his arguments than the basically theological problem he sets out to solve in the fourth meditation.

Descartes' proffered solution to the problem of error turns on his conception of the intellect, of our understanding, of that part of the mind that differs from the will, as a kind of internal arena in which ideas present themselves as neutral contents that remain neutral until we make judgments about them: that is, until we assent to the ideas as true representations or reject them as false, illusory, or self-generated as when we imagine something. In perception of the world around us, therefore, to perceive something is first to have an idea that is in itself neutral and second to assent to the idea. What we assent to are ideas as representational – literally, as picturing what they are ideas of, their causes. If we are right and have not judged hastily, the combination of the ideas entertained and our judgments, our assent to the ideas, jointly constitute perception of things around us.

An idea of a table, for example, is initially in the mind the way a dollar bill is in my pocket. So long as I do not try to do anything with the piece of engraved paper in my pocket – spend the dollar – it remains neutral. It is only when I try to buy something with the bill that its authenticity as legal tender becomes an issue and the possibility arises that it may be counterfeit. In the same way, mere awareness of the idea of a table, which seems to be an idea of a material, extended object, is just that: an idea present to the mind. When I try to do something with or to the table, it is like trying to spend the dollar bill. If I try to place something on the table, I assent to the idea as a representation of a real table, just as when I hand over the dollar bill in a transaction I judge that it is legal tender and not counterfeit. If the table supports what I place on it, my judgment that my idea of it is an accurate representation appears to be confirmed because what I place on the table does not fall through what then would turn out to be only an imagined or hallucinated table. Though judgment might occur in a more abstract manner, typically it is when I go to put something on the table or perhaps try to move it that I assent to the idea of the table as being of a material, extended object, and so my having the idea becomes perception of a table.

The problem with Descartes' account of perception as the entertaining of ideas and assenting to some has two parts. The first part is that we are not aware of any such two-step process; instead we experience only immediate awareness of physical things around us – even though we are sometimes wrong. And given Descartes' conception of the mind as transparent to itself, of everything that is thought being conscious thought, the two-step process should be accessible to us when we attend carefully to instances of perception. The elusivity of the process makes it look like Descartes invents and imposes the two-step process precisely in order to be able to explain error as the process going wrong due to our impetuousness.

The second part of the problem is that even if we were to accept the two-step process, if only for the argument's sake, the assenting to an idea as a representation of an actual table does not of itself establish that the supposed cause of the idea, the material object, actually exists. Confirmation of the judgment that the idea of a table represents a table, such as placing something on the table and having that something be supported by what appears to be the table, is only evidence for the conjecture that there really is a table there. It is possible, for example, that I hallucinate something's being supported by the table just as I hallucinate the table itself. This is the epistemological bind that Descartes and others never get out of: we can pile up evidence about the nature and existence of external objects but it never reaches the point of conclusiveness. The actual existence of things outside our minds, of things only conveyed to our minds by ideas, must remain conjectural no matter how much evidence there might be. This is because all we have direct access to in Descartes' conception of mind are our own ideas. We never can get beyond our ideas to the things themselves, since they are always experienced indirectly through ideas. That is why it is necessary for Descartes to offer a general argument for the existence of matter in the sixth meditation.

* * *

It is worth mentioning that the implausibility of Descartes' understanding of perception as a two-step process may appear to be mitigated for contemporary readers of the *Meditations* by the impression that the oddness of Descartes' two-step process is due only to his account being an early anticipation of the complexity of the present-day neurophysiological account of perception. However, this impression is seriously mistaken. What needs to be appreciated is that Descartes' position is not just that we do not perceive things like trees and tables directly and that their perception involves a process of which we are not conscious. That much is compatible with what we now know about the neural processes involved in sense-perception and about the impact on the senses of light-waves and sound-waves. The trouble is that for Descartes, every potential representation we experience being individually attended to as a neutral idea and then being judged to be a representation of a real thing, of its cause, is a sequence of mental acts, not of causal events. The two-step process Descartes describes is a thought-process; it is not a physical and neural one. As far as Descartes is concerned, the physical and neural goings-on that contemporary accounts of perception describe are events in a material body the existence of which has yet to be demonstrated. There is, therefore, no parallel between Descartes' two-step process and what goes on when light or sound impinge on our retinas or eardrums and initiate complex neural sequences.

Note that the preceding discussion's focus on perception follows on Descartes' own focus; that is, I am not myself picking out perception as the weak point in his argument. It is true that his account of how error occurs is not limited to perception, that it applies equally to reasoning in that premises and conclusions may be assented to precipitously or on inadequate bases. However, it is less clear how the elements of reasoning are present to the mind as ideas to assent to or otherwise, hence how the will prompts hasty assent. This is the issue we encountered before of how what is essentially propositional is presented to the mind as so many ideas, and it is not an issue that is resolved or even clarified in the fourth meditation.

SUMMARY

Descartes' explanation of how error occurs, and hence of why error is not God's fault for creating human beings with perfect wills but only adequate intellects, amounts to claiming that our perfectly free wills improperly override our adequate intellects, our limited understanding. The explanation turns on two notions, both of which are implausible, albeit for different reasons. The first notion is that we have perfectly free will; the second is Descartes' two-step account of perception as involving the entertaining of ideas and the assenting to or rejecting of those ideas.

The notion of perfect will, though highly important in ethical and theological contexts, is somewhat surprisingly of secondary importance in the fourth meditation. The reason seems to be that we find the very concept puzzling and ill-defined at least to the extent that the sense of 'perfectly free' is left too vague and nothing is offered by way of criteria useful for establishing when a will is or is not free in the requisite sense.

The two-step account of perception, once it is clearly seen to be an account of a wholly mental process, seems to be more an *ad hoc* devise, convenient for quelling the fear that God might be blamed for error, than a serious philosophical explanation. The main reason for this is the inaccessibility of a process that we supposedly engage in deliberately.

As a result, the fourth meditation is of greater philosophical significance for what it tells us and implies about Descartes' understanding of perception and the structure of the mind, than for its ingenious but unconvincing explanation of how errors of judgment arise.

CHAPTER 8

THE FIFTH MEDITATION: THE ONTOLOGICAL ARGUMENT FOR GOD'S EXISTENCE

The fifth meditation's main point is to prove the existence of God by appealing to reason alone; there is no appeal to experience as there is in the causal argument offered in the third meditation. Anselm's original Ontological argument and Descartes' version of it are purely conceptual; the basic contention is that the concept of God suffices to prove God's existence in that the concept necessitates that God exist in the sense that the concept would be incoherent if God did not, in fact, exist. Contrary to this, the third meditation's causal argument relies on a principle different from the concept of God itself, because Descartes maintains that it is our experience of having the idea of a perfect God that leads us to conclude that only a perfect God can be the cause of the idea.

A clarification needs to be made before we proceed with the fifth meditation's argument. Some readers may be tempted to think that the Ontological argument's point is that if we have the concept of a perfect God, that what the nature of the concept necessitates is that we assent to the idea of God as existent. In other words, you may think that the argument's conclusion is that when we entertain the concept of God, and understand it, we must accept that God exists. This is not quite right because the force of the Ontological argument has to do with existence, not with assent or belief regarding existence. The point is that Anselm and Descartes' contention is that the very concept of God as perfect necessitates that the concept is, in fact, instantiated. Differently put, when we grasp the concept of a perfect God, we realize that what we have grasped is that there is a perfect God, that God actually exists. The difference here is a little elusive, but it is a real one between our only accepting that we have to believe God exists, and our understanding that God does exist, must exist, whether we believe it or not.

The argument offered in the fifth meditation, then, purports to establish the actual existence of God by appealing only to the concept of God. As does Anselm's Ontological argument, Descartes' argument purports to show that the concept of God is of such a nature that it entails instantiation: that is, the concept is such that it must and can only be the concept of an actually existent being rather than only of a possibly existent one.

There is something of a parallel here to Descartes' derivation of the concept of extension or matter. Descartes' point regarding matter is that once we have the concept of matter, we understand that while there may be no matter at all, if there is matter it must be extended. The experiment with the wax captures the essence of matter by showing its defining characteristic, namely, extension; but the question of whether matter actually exists remains open and is left for the sixth meditation. What Descartes is after in the fifth meditation is a similar point regarding God's defining properties, but inspired by Anselm he maintains that in the case of God, unlike in the case of matter, the defining properties the concept encompasses do of themselves entail existence. In our own time this contention would be immediately rejected as confusedly holding a relation of entailment between thought or something propositional and something existent in the world. We do not accept that logical relations hold between anything but propositions, but neither Descartes nor Anselm held this to be the case; for both there is a relation of entailment between the concept of God and the existence of God.

Given Descartes' preparedness to see an entailment relation between the concept of God and God's actual existence in the fifth meditation, it is unclear why the idea of God is used in the third meditation as an object of experience and the basis for a causal argument, while in the fifth meditation the concept of God suffices to prove God's existence. This lack of clarity suggests that likely Descartes' causal argument collapses into the Ontological one, but the lack of clarity also prompts a more significant question about why Descartes feels the need to offer two arguments for the existence of God.

* * *

What is supposed to differentiate the arguments offered in the third and the fifth meditations is that the former is an *a posteriori* argument and the latter is *a priori* one. The reason the former is *a posteriori* or dependent on experience is because its ground is our experience of having the idea of God. The reason the latter is *a priori* is because its conclusion follows purely from reasoned reflection on the concept of God. The possibility that the supposedly causal argument collapses into the *a priori* one turns on whether Descartes can consistently and convincingly maintain that having the idea of God is a matter of experience, while having the concept of God is not.

The *a priori* nature of the Ontological argument means that both Descartes' and Anselm's arguments are essentially the same. To refer to Descartes' argument as a version of Anselm's is a bit of an overstatement. There really is only one Ontological argument, though there are somewhat different articulations of it. Descartes' articulation of the argument is perhaps the briefest, but whatever articulation or version is considered, you must pay close attention to the precise language used because it is crucial to see that the argument turns on conception and not understanding in a more inclusive sense. That is, the argument is about understanding the word 'God' as meaning or referring to the entity with every perfection, not about understanding God in the looser sense we often use when we say someone understands something, which usually includes several levels of familiarity with whatever is said to be understood. Many beginners confuse the notion of conception used in the Ontological argument with the more common usage of understanding that includes being able to imagine what is understood. When Anselm and Descartes speak of understanding the concept of God, they mean no more than what one gains when one looks up a word in a dictionary. More specifically, they mean that in having or understanding the concept of God, one grasps that God is the perfect being, that God is, in Anselm's original formulation, 'that than which no greater can be conceived.'

Many beginners also get confused about the conceptual force of the Ontological argument, thinking that Descartes or Anselm is imposing on them some particular theological understanding of God. That is not the case. The only thing Descartes is appealing to, following Anselm, is conception of God as wholly perfect. If someone has a conception of God as less than perfect, whether as still in the process of becoming perfect or as lacking certain perfections, then the Ontological argument simply does not apply to that conception. The argument is specifically about the conception of God as perfect, as having every perfection, as perfect in every possible way. The argument, though flawed in a number of ways, does not presuppose a particular theologically specific understanding of God – for instance, as having created the world in a particular way, as requiring particular sorts of worship, or as promising a particular kind of afterlife. The Ontological argument turns only on God's perfection, not on particular articles of faith regarding divine demands, entitlements, and assurances. The argument requires only that possession of the concept of a perfect God enables the understanding of phrases like 'the perfect being' or 'the greatest conceivable being' or 'a being lacking no perfection.'

* * *

As Descartes presents it, the Ontological argument is that to entertain the concept of the perfect God in the intellect, and to think God nonexistent or only possibly existent – in other words to fail to assent to the idea as representational and veridical – is to contradict oneself. This again raises the issue of how a concept can entail existence, and to appreciate how Descartes thinks this works, we need to consider one of his fundamental presuppositions: a presupposition that he shares with Anselm and seems never to examine critically.

The presupposition is that existence is a property, and a positive property, so existence is a property that God must possess in perfect measure, just as God possesses omniscience, omnipotence, and benevolence in perfect measure. Existence, then, is a perfection. To think of God is to think of a divine entity with every perfection, therefore to think of God simply in having and reflecting on the concept of God is to think of God as existent. To think of God as only an idea, as only possibly existent, or as nonexistent, is to think of the divine entity with every perfection as lacking at least one perfection – existence – and that is contradictory. Note that here one may be tempted to think that what is at issue is only acceptance of God as existing; but as considered earlier, that is not what is at issue. The point is that to have and reflect on the concept of the perfect God is to understand, to realize, that God does exist.

In Anselm's presentation of the Ontological argument, he refers to the biblical fool who said 'in his heart' that there is no God, while understanding the concept, which is what makes him a fool. For the fool to deny the existence of God is to think of God, as the subject of the denial; it is to entertain the concept of God. That is in itself to think of a divine entity that is perfect and so necessarily has existence as one of its perfections. It also is to then immediately deny existence to that divine entity. In other words, to think of God and to deny God's existence is to at once attribute existence to God, just by reflecting on the concept, and at the same time to deny God's existence, in saying God does not exist. For Anselm and Descartes, that is just like saying 'It's raining but it's not raining'; it is to contradict oneself.

* * *

The basic problem with the Ontological argument is that it tries to move from conception to reality; from concepts to what they are concepts of. For Descartes' the move is justified by his understanding of existence as being a property, and as such as necessarily being possessed by the one entity that has – and must have – every positive property in perfect measure. Both Hume and Kant challenged Descartes' presupposition that existence is a property. Hume pointed out that if I entertain the idea of a thing, I add nothing to the idea if I then think of the thing as existing. Kant's argument is more complex, but its point is the same: existence is not a property; existence is not something possessed, therefore possession of existence is not a perfection and existence is not one of the properties necessarily possessed by a purportedly perfect God.

With respect to Anselm's original formulation of the Ontological argument, one of Anselm's contemporaries, a monk named

Gaunilo, argued against Anselm that if the Ontological argument did work, it could be used to prove the existence of anything we might think of as perfect, for example, a perfect island. At first glance it will seem that Gaunilo's counterargument does not work, because the idea of a perfect island is quite different from the idea of a perfect God in that a perfect island's properties would be more limited in kind and number than those of a perfect God, and could not include volitional attributes such as omnipotence or benevolence. However, recall that Anselm's argument turns on God having every perfection and being that than which no greater can be conceived. God's perfections are not specified. Gaunilo's point would be that all we need to do in the island case is narrow the reference: instead of 'that' than which no greater can be conceived, we would say 'that island' than which no greater can be conceived.

However, whether Gaunilo's counterargument does or does not work, what it brings out is that Anselm assumes too much when he blithely asserts that we do in fact have the concept of a perfect God. This is precisely the same problem Descartes faces with regard to his causal argument for God's existence by assuming that we do have the idea of a perfect God – and note that Descartes' assumption also was challenged by his contemporaries. Whether it is Anselm's or Descartes' articulation of the Ontological argument, either would be more plausible if we could say more about God's perfection. But when we examine the too-vaguely inclusive claim that God has every perfection, we realize that we really do not understand what is being claimed. For one thing, we have no idea about how God's various perfections relate one to another: recall the point made earlier about the tensions in attributing to God perfect justice and perfect mercy.

Descartes does think the argument proceeds without difficulty, contending it to be 'manifest' that we cannot separate God's essence and God's existence. Descartes is convinced that the former entails the latter, and that they cannot be separated any more than we can separate from the concept of a rectilinear triangle the fact that its internal angles equal 180 degrees (Descartes 5, 63 [I, 181]).

* * *

Descartes' articulation of the Ontological argument, as it is presented in the fifth meditation, raises a question that is of some significance, though it is not one often considered in historical or expository works about Descartes. The question is why Descartes offers two arguments for the existence of God. In spite of the brevity of the *Meditations*, Descartes finds it necessary to devote two of his meditations to two different arguments for God's existence. The reason this is an issue is that considering how Descartes attempts to emulate geometric arguments and proofs in his philosophizing, it seems somewhat peculiar that he offers two proofs for God's existence. First of all, offering two arguments for the same conclusion violates the elegance of geometric proofs by introducing redundancy; but more serious is that by providing two arguments for the same conclusion Descartes weakens both arguments by suggesting that neither is sufficient by itself.

In addition to Descartes' puzzling presentation of two arguments for God's existence, one or the other of which should be superfluous if each is as solid as we are led to believe, the Ontological argument was well known long before Descartes and as we saw in Chapter 6 was criticized by no less than Aquinas as presuming more positive knowledge of God's nature than finite beings can achieve. Given all he says about not relying on tradition and authority and about establishing conclusions with certainty through rigorous argumentation, Descartes' inclusion of the Ontological argument in addition to his own original causal argument does look a little suspicious.

Descartes himself says little about his reasons for offering two arguments for God's existence, but the little he does say is suggestive. Near the end of his response to the first set of objections to his *Meditations*, Descartes remarks that there are only two ways of proving the existence of God, one is 'by means of the effects due to him,' as supposedly established in the third meditation's causal argument, and the other is by reflection on God's 'essence or nature,' which is what the Ontological argument in the fifth meditation is all about (Descartes, *Reply to Objections I*, Haldane and Ross 1969, Vol. II, 22). What Descartes says in replying to the objections does suggest that perhaps he is merely meeting expectations regarding presentation of the well-known Ontological argument. That is, it may be that Descartes thinks ignoring the Ontological argument might seem questionable to his more theologically inclined peers, and that his inclusion of it in the *Meditations* is more *pro forma* than it is a philosophically prompted move.

My own view of Descartes' reason for including the Ontological argument is that he has what I will describe as a basically procedural reason for including both the causal argument of the third meditation, which in appealing to our actual possession of the idea of God appeals to experience, and the Ontological argument of the fifth meditation, which appeals only to grasp of the concept of God. The reason has to do with how in developing his methodological doubt Descartes offers two hypotheses, the dream hypothesis and the evil-spirit hypothesis, to separately impugn ideas deriving from experience, on the one hand, and truths of reason on the other. It seems proper procedure, then, to establish the existence of God in both ways: on the basis of experience and on the basis of reason alone. Having drawn the distinction, if only by producing the dream and evil-spirit hypotheses, Descartes likely felt obliged to offer an *a posteriori* argument for God's existence as well as an *a priori* one to show that God's existence is demonstrable regardless of whether we rely on experience or on reason.

If my interpretation is correct, the important point is that God emerges as the only thing capable of wholly conclusive argumentative proof on the basis of experience or of reason. The conclusiveness of the *cogito* intuition is not due to valid argumentation but to direct realization that thinking or doubting necessarily manifests existence. As for the existence of extended matter, as we will see in the next chapter, that demonstration is not conclusive because establishment of the existence of matter is mediated by God's goodness. God's existence, then, is the only reality that can be demonstrated directly through argument, whether it be a causal or *a posteriori* argument or a conceptual or *a priori* one. This would strike Descartes as an important point, hence his provision of the two arguments.

SUMMARY

The key to understanding the argument for God's existence in the fifth meditation is to first understand what it means to have a concept. A concept is, at base, a recognitional capacity. If someone has the concept 'tree,' say, it means that someone can recognize something as being a tree or not being a tree. An elm or oak, for instance would be recognized as a tree, and likely as a tree of a particular type, whereas a lilac bush would be recognized as not a tree though tree-like in certain respects. In more abstract cases, having a concept is the capacity to recognize something under a particular description, for instance understanding that a physical act, such as taking some money out of a drawer, may be a moral act – in this case the immoral act of theft. A more rarefied example is having the concept of epistemology, say, and so having the capacity to understand that Descartes' questions about the existence of matter are not practical queries about whether there is something there or not, but are part of the effort to determine what can be known about the world as opposed to what is only believed about the contents of sensory perception.

With all concepts we are able to give at least minimal criteria for something to fall under the concept, of what it is to be a tree, a bush, a moral act, an instance of knowledge, or a unicorn – and this last is important because what concepts are concepts of need not actually exist or may no longer exist or might not yet exist. For example we understand what a centaur is even though centaurs are mythical; we understand what a dodo was even though there are no more dodos; and we understand what teleportation would be even if it is not yet possible.

What Anselm and Descartes contend is that we understand what a perfect God is, not because – as Aquinas worried – we have knowledge of God's attributes or nature, but because we understand that God has every perfection, that God has every positive attribute or property, such as goodness and knowledge, and has those attributes or properties in infinite or perfect measure. So if God has knowledge, God is omniscient; if God is good, God is all-good or good without exception or qualification. The concept of a perfect God just is the concept of the greatest conceivable being, of the being than which no greater can be conceived. And to grasp the concept we need not consider specific properties or attributes, like goodness or knowledge. All we have to understand is that God has every perfection and is the end-point in conceivability; that unlike an infinite series, where we can always add one, in the case of God we cannot add perfections; God is the terminus of perfection.

The next crucial point is the one disputed by Hume and Kant, namely, that existence is a property or attribute as goodness and knowledge are attributes or properties. The idea is that God – and anything that exists – actually has existence in the sense that the property of existence is possessed.

Once existence is conceived as being a property, it follows necessarily that since it is a positive property – it is better to exist than not to exist – God has to have that property. That is what the Ontological argument is designed to establish: God is perfect in that God has every positive property, therefore God has existence.

I hope that about now you are experiencing a certain reservation which, if you indeed are having it, indicates growing philosophical sophistication. Notice that in this summary and in other parts of the chapter reference is made to positive properties and, more specifically, to existence as a positive property. You may be wondering where that comes from in the sense that it is not explicitly argued for in Descartes' presentation of either the causal or the Ontological argument.

The reservation is sound because Descartes does assume that we can differentiate straightforwardly between positive and negative properties with respect to God, and he also assumes that existence is better than nonexistence. The latter point may be arguable, but it is not of major concern here; it is the former point that looms large in both the causal and Ontological arguments for God's existence. Aquinas' reservations about the Ontological argument presupposing too great a knowledge of God's nature were justified. Descartes offers a list of familiar divine attributes, most notably omniscience, omnipotence, and benevolence. But the list raises questions. Consider a moment: is not benevolence, to take one divine attribute, an attribute cast in our own image? In fact, are not most of the perfections Descartes lists as possessed by God not anthropomorphic? The perfections he attributes to God are very much those we value most; are they necessarily the attributes of an infinite being? However, interesting as all of this might be, it is for you to consider when you have the opportunity. Now we must proceed to learning – at long last – whether or not the material world is real.

CHAPTER 9

THE SIXTH MEDITATION: THE WORLD'S EXISTENCE

The sixth meditation is where Descartes attempts to fulfill his implicit promise to establish that the concept of matter, which is derived in the second meditation, is instantiated: that extended substance actually exists. Establishing the existence of matter must wait until the sixth meditation because it is first necessary for Descartes to prove the existence of God, and moreover the existence of a perfect God that is all-good or benevolent and not a deceiver. It is absolutely crucial to the argument for matter's existence that God not have need or desire to deceive us, that God does not deceive us because doing so is wholly alien to God's essential nature. As will emerge, though Descartes does not say so explicitly, it is necessary to completely rule out the possibility that we are dreaming when we take it we perceive material objects, but especially that we are not fooled by an evil spirit into thinking we perceive material objects when there is nothing there but ideas presented to our minds.

The possibility that we are only dreaming the physical things we think we see and touch supposedly has been taken care of by Descartes' emphasis on the difference between the waking and dreaming states in terms of detail, continuity, and particularly our deep conviction about the contents of our sensory awareness. At a practical level, this seems enough to quell our fears about only dreaming what we think we see, hear, and feel. At the level Descartes is supposedly operating, it does not seem enough to lay to rest the dream hypothesis. But whether it is or is not enough, the evil-spirit hypothesis has not been adequately dealt with; in fact, it seems not to have been dealt with at all until we reflect on what Descartes believes he accomplishes in the third meditation. As was alluded to earlier and will emerge more clearly hereafter, how the evil spirit is banished is not only a little complicated, it is an entirely tacit matter because of theological – we might say ideological – risks involved in Descartes being explicit about why the evil spirit does not pose a problem for the establishment of the existence of extended matter.

* * *

The first thing to understand about the supposed proof of the reality of the external world offered in the sixth meditation is that it is not a proof at all. You need to appreciate that even if Descartes' argument for the existence of matter were flawless, it would not constitute a demonstration of matter's existence, and of course it neither is nor can be an intuition like the *cogito*. The reason was referred to earlier and is that matter can never be known directly the way mind supposedly is known directly as a substance through exercise of its defining property, thought.

The lack of direct access to matter inherent in Descartes' conception of mind enabled Bishop George Berkeley (1685–1753), an empiricist and contemporary of Locke and Hume, to deny matter's independent existence, arguing that actual, existent matter would be superfluous to ideas and that God would not create a superfluous substance. Berkeley argued for idealism or the view that mind – including the divine Mind – and ideas present to mind are all that exist; he summed up his position in the dictum 'to be is to be perceived,' meaning that to exist simply is to be present to a mind as an idea (Matson 2000, 395–410).

Berkeley and idealism aside, the important thing is that because extension cannot be known directly, as is made clear in the second meditation where Descartes derives the concept of extension from his wax example, there always must be an inferential step in any argument for matter's existence: a step that in one or another way carries us from our ideas of things to the inferred actuality of the things themselves. However, as we will see hereafter, Descartes cannot make that step without God's perfect goodness and consequent unwillingness to deceive us.

Before we proceed to consider the argument we need to reconsider the evil-spirit hypothesis to better understand Descartes' thinking. As he frames the evil-spirit hypotheses, the spirit deceives us deliberately, not because it needs to in order to accomplish some other end, but as an end in itself. This is what makes the evil spirit evil: deliberate deception. The problem that arises with the hypothesis is posed by the fact that the evil spirit must have great power to fool us about truths of reason and to do so consistently and effectively and in ways that do not even allow us to imagine how what we believe might be otherwise. Recall that as was pointed out in the example used in Chapter 3, we cannot imagine how five and five could be anything but ten, yet must consider that we are deceived into thinking that five and five do equal ten when that is – somehow – false.

It is inevitable to think that the evil spirit's power must be god-like power, which leads to a dilemma: one horn is that God allows the evil spirit to have great power to deceive or even gave the spirit that power; the other horn is the more likely possibility that what Descartes actually postulates – at least temporarily – in his evil-spirit hypothesis is that God deceives us about truths of reason. But since the evil spirit is evil precisely in that it deceives us deliberately and maliciously, Descartes cannot explicitly suggest even temporarily that it is God who deceives, as that would be blasphemous and highly offensive to his audience. However, if the second possibility remains tacit; if there is no explicit reference to God but only to an evil spirit, Descartes gets away with the postulation. And what makes it seem very likely that Descartes does have God in mind when he puts forward the evil-spirit hypothesis is that as soon as God is described in the third meditation as perfect – and so all-good and not deceptive – the evil spirit ceases to be a considered possibility. The issue of divine deception only arises again in the sixth meditation, but there it is its impossibility that is focused on and becomes the force behind the argument for matter's existence.

Notice that there is a larger issue in the background when we consider Descartes' insistence that a perfect God does not deceive us. That issue is how omnipotence and benevolence interact or balance one another as divine attributes. Surely God's omnipotence must be restricted to some degree by the obligation arising from perfect benevolence to not deceive us, even indirectly. This is essentially the same question raised earlier about how perfect justice and perfect mercy interact or balance one another as divine attributes, and one indication of its seriousness are the lengths Descartes goes to in the fourth meditation to remove any hint of divine responsibility for errors of judgment. However, I leave it to you to speculate about this point; we now need to consider the purported establishment of matter's existence.

* * *

Turning to the argument itself, Descartes begins by stressing the degree of conviction he feels when he has ideas that present themselves as being of physical things in the world external to his mind. He is careful to remain within the bounds of his ideas, contending only that his conviction is that some ideas truly represent things which are not themselves ideas. Descartes does not claim to be convinced that he senses things themselves; only that some objects of awareness, objects in the sense of ideas having objective reality in being present to his mind, are caused by things with actual reality outside his mind – and it is important to understanding the sixth meditation to keep in mind how Descartes called 'objective' what we call 'subjective.'

The point of departure for the sixth meditation's argument is reiteration that the contents of Descartes' awareness consist of ideas, of objects of thought. The issue is whether some ideas truly represent things external to the mind; whether some objects of thought are ideational portraits of things having actual reality in their own right. This is the question whether extended substance or matter exists.

The gist of the argument Descartes offers is this: there is a marked difference among his ideas. Some, like the idea of a unicorn, do not prompt the conviction in him that they are caused representations of things external to his mind; others, like the idea of his own hand, decidedly do prompt the conviction that they represent real things. These latter objects of thought present themselves as caused by things having actual, in-the-world reality, and they do so strongly enough that Descartes needed to produce the dream hypothesis to question their representational veracity as part of his methodological doubt. The question then is: how might his conviction be wrong? What would it take for Descartes to have this conviction but for the ideas he takes as representing real things not to represent real things?

This is where Descartes – knowingly or unknowingly – gives his argument a decidedly moral twist. It seems the only thing that could explain Descartes being wrong about his firm conviction regarding some of his ideas representing actually real things is God deceiving him. But the God proven to exist in the third and fifth meditations is a perfect God, therefore not a deceiver. Descartes' deep conviction, then, must be true and if it is true it follows that matter exists as the cause of the ideas he firmly believes are of things external to his mind.

The moral twist to the argument is not only the obvious point that God does not deceive Descartes about the actual reality of extended matter because it is wrong to deceive, to lie. The less obvious point to the moral twist is that Descartes presents his conviction that many of his ideas are veridical representations of their causes as if his having that conviction ultimately is God's doing in that God created him with the faculties and inclinations he has. So if his having the conviction ultimately is God's doing, then God must have created matter because otherwise the conviction would be a deception. Differently put, Descartes is putting a moral burden on how the content of our sensory awareness is presented to us as perception of real things independent of our minds. He is, in effect, saying: If God created me so that I firmly believe that most of what I see, hear, smell, taste, and feel is real and not just in my mind, then unless God is a deceiver, which we know God is not, there must be real things out there that I see, hear, smell, taste, and feel.

Notice that there is here, if not an inconsistency then at least a tension with the argument of the fourth meditation. There we are told that error is not God's fault because we make hasty judgments due to our wills outstripping our intellects. There we are cautioned to be scrupulous in weighing and testing our inclinations and convictions in order to be judicious in assenting to something as true. Why then is it the case that convictions of veracity about sensory perception, which are due only to the force and vivacity of presentation of the ideas, suddenly override the need for the thorough assessment that insures judicious assent? The answer seems to be that God created us so that we experience the contents of sensory perception with great force and vivacity, and since God does not and would not deceive us, we can trust our convictions about the veracity of ideas of things in the world. We may have to allow for occasional exceptions, but that has to do with particular apparent perceptions, not with perception of the physical world as such. It seems, then, that we are right to trust our senses except when we are wrong to trust them.

* * *

Descartes' argument for the existence of matter raises significant philosophical and theological issues. The salient philosophical issue is that establishing the representational veracity of the ideas of things external to the mind is irreducibly inferential, unlike the intuition of our own existence and, supposedly, the proof of God's existence. The external causes of ideas of material things never can be known directly, so Descartes' conviction that some ideas represent actual realities can never reach the degree of certainty of the *cogito* intuition: it can never match his paradigm of truth. The implications of our only having mediated access to extended substance, however worrying for Descartes, are devastating for subsequent philosophical thinkers because they vitiate epistemology. To paraphrase Foucault, the implications make Hume possible, and Hume makes knowledge of the world impossible (Foucault 1973, 60).

The theologically salient issue, considered earlier, involves the initial introduction of the evil spirit and the evil spirit's convenient disappearance after the third meditation. The basic point is this: when Descartes introduces the evil spirit, it is hard not to think that he is postulating that God may be deceiving us – however temporarily. There seems insufficient reason to postulate the existence of another greatly powerful entity characterized by nothing else than the desire to deceive Descartes about truths of reason. Of course Descartes cannot say that God might deceive him without outraging the Faculty of Theology he was so concerned to please, as well as offending most of his contemporaries, so the evil spirit is presented as a strategic fiction.

An alternative open to Descartes is to present the evil spirit as Satan, and to contend that despite being all-good, God tolerates Satan's deception of us regarding sensory perception as God tolerates Satan's tempting us to sin. This alternative is in line with theological thinking, but if Descartes takes it, he compromises the argument of the sixth meditation. The reason is that the argument turns precisely on God not allowing Descartes to be deceived about those things that he believes with the described degree of conviction.

The upshot is a different version of the dilemma considered earlier: either the evil-spirit hypothesis turns out to be a hypothesis in which it is implicit that God deceives Descartes, and the 'evil spirit' evaporates when God emerges in the third meditation as perfect and therefore nondeceptive, or the evil spirit is Satan and tolerated by God for divine reasons about which we can only speculate. The problem with the first horn of the dilemma is that it is blasphemous; the problem with the second horn is that if the evil spirit is Satan, and hence continues to exist as at least a potential deceiver, the argument for the existence of matter is compromised because it depends on our not being deceived by a higher power about our firm convictions regarding the veracity of sensory ideas.

What concerns us most is the philosophical issue, and to fully appreciate it we need to place it in the context of the major epistemological implications of Descartes' conception of the mind. The key implication is that all our knowledge of the world external to the mind, if there is indeed a material world, is gained through ideas, so the actual reality of anything extended is always inferred on the basis of the objective reality of ideas. That is why the sixth meditation's argument for the actual reality of material things, which is so apparently evident in the forceful objective reality of some ideas, essentially is that what guarantees the veracity of ideas about things in the world precisely is that only divine deception could make that evident reality false, and there is no divine deception.

* * *

As pointed out in the previous chapter, given the inferential epistemological structure of our awareness of extended matter, aside from our own existence which is directly intuited, God is the only thing the existence of which Descartes can demonstrate conclusively solely on the basis of ideas themselves. This is because only a perfect God can be the cause of the idea of a perfect God, and because the idea – the concept – of a perfect God entails existence. The existence of matter, however, is forever inferential because our access to extended matter is only through its depiction in our ideas.

The foregoing point can be put in terms of substances in a way that brings out an issue that haunts Cartesian thinking, which is how there can be interaction between different substances. We are mental substances the defining property of which is thought. As mental substances, we cannot have direct awareness of material substance, the defining property of which is extension – put in contemporary terms, mind is nonspatial by nature and matter is spatial by nature. What we as mental substances have are ideas that represent material substance, but ideas are, of course, mental in being thoughts present to the mind. Therefore, without direct access to material substance, our belief that it exists and any beliefs we have about it rest entirely on our ideas. To establish that material substance exists, we only have recourse to the trustworthiness of those of our ideas which we take as sensory representations. The way that trustworthiness is supported is that Descartes argues that our ideas of material substance are so firmly believed by us that they must be true unless God deceives us. God, though, is perfect and all-good, so does not deceive us, therefore material substance exists as we believe it does.

SUMMARY

The sixth meditation makes abundantly clear the progression of Descartes' arguments as well as why his arguments progress as they do. He begins with skepticism in the first meditation and then establishes his own existence in the second. However, what is crucial is that he establishes his own existence as a thing that thinks, as a mental substance. It then follows from the *cogito* intuition that everything else Descartes thinks exists differs fundamentally from what he is as a thing that thinks or as a substance defined by thought. God, of course, is divine and so is utterly different in kind. Matter is substance defined by extension, and differs completely from mind. What concerns us about the difference between divine substance and extended substance is that the existence of divine substance, of God, is conclusively provable by reason and experience or by reason alone, whereas the existence of extended substance, of matter, is, as it were, another matter.

Matter's existence cannot be conclusively proven by reason or experience because we have access to it only through ideas that represent it. In Descartes' own terms, the actual reality of extended matter is available to us only through the objective reality of the ideational copies of it presented to our minds. How Descartes deals with this problem is by stressing the depth of our convictions about the veracity of – most – of the ideas that seem to be representations of extended matter. He focuses our attention on how thoroughly and systematically we take for granted the contents of sensory awareness and how – for the most part – doing so works just fine. The picture he paints, then, is of us as so sure that matter exists that the only way we could be wrong, the only reason all our ideas of things external to our minds might be false and nothing exist beyond our ideas, is that God deceives us. God, though, has twice been proven not only to exist but to be perfect and therefore to be all-good and so not a deceiver. The sixth meditation's point, therefore, is that since God does not deceive us about it, extended matter must exist as we firmly believe it does.

The trouble is the 'must' in the last sentence. If we drop it and just say matter exists, we go beyond what is strictly correct because matter's existence is contingent, first on God's existence and second on God's perfection and thus unpreparedness to deceive. As far as Descartes is concerned, the existence of matter follows as a sound conclusion from the premises stating God's existence and perfect goodness, but the soundness of that conclusion is dependent on the truth of the premises, and problems with the idea of perfection and with conception of existence as a property render those premises problematic enough that the conclusion remains problematic.

CHAPTER 10

CONCLUSION

This closing chapter is in three parts: in the first part I continue with the recapitulation of the *Meditations* promised at the end of Chapter 9; in the second part I relate the major points of Descartes' thought to some contemporary philosophical developments, as promised in Chapter 1; and in the third part I offer a short essay-type account of the events in Descartes' life most relevant to an introduction to his work. To begin, I return to where we found ourselves at the end of the sixth meditation.

OVERVIEW OF THE MEDITATIONS

Supposedly, at the end of the sixth meditation, everything is as it was before the implementation of methodological doubt, except that all Descartes only believed when he began to apply his methodological doubt has now been demonstrated to be true as opposed to only believed or taken for granted by him. Descartes does not claim to discover anything new in his meditations, with the possible exception of his causal argument for God's existence; instead, he claims to establish the veracity of what he previously only accepted unreflectively as being the case.

At the end of the *Meditations*, then, Descartes supposedly has discerned and articulated philosophically sound reasons for holding what he always believed: that he himself exists; that God exists; and that the world exists. He need not fear that he is dreaming or is being deceived by an evil spirit. Additionally, as part of the process of establishing truths about his own existence and about God's existence, he has come to understand and to articulate how he, not God, bears the responsibility for errors in reasoning and perception. The far-reaching bonus of the six meditations is that by establishing the veracity of his beliefs in his own existence, God's existence, and the existence of the external world, Descartes takes himself to have formulated the basic methodological principles and fundamental truths that ground all human knowledge and any further development of it.

The reality is rather different. What Descartes actually succeeds in doing in his meditations is to open an unbridgeable gulf between consciousness and the world. He succeeds in isolating himself – and us – as minds defined by the intrinsic property of thought but therefore categorically separated from all that is defined by the property of extension. From the point in the second meditation when mental substance is defined and separated in nature from extended substance, things external to the mind recede into an epistemologically inaccessible dimension. The world is made unreachable and our belief in its reality comes to rest precariously on the nondeceptiveness of a God whose existence is not conclusively proven. Moreover, the distinction between substances that makes the world epistemologically problematic has another negative consequence: rather than providing a methodology and a certain basis for the development of human knowledge, what actually ensued in the wake of the *Meditations* was a number of unworkable philosophical positions. The most notable of these were dualism, with its attendant insurmountable problems regarding the epistemological and ontological gaps between mind and matter, and idealism, the intellectually and certainly practically sterile ontological and epistemological reduction of matter to mind.

As for the rest, what was least in doubt, his own existence, is the only thing Descartes establishes successfully. The existence of God remains problematic because neither the causal argument nor the Ontological argument is compelling – except to those who already believe in God. The idea of a perfect God eludes us, thus subverting the third meditation's causal argument, and existence not being a property vitiates the fifth meditation's Ontological argument.

As for the explanation of error in the fourth meditation, it is unnecessary, contrived, and in any case too narrow in scope with respect to error, not all of which is a function of rash judgment. Lastly, not only is the establishment of matters' existence left irreducibly inferential, it ultimately rests on the goodness of a God the benevolence and especially the existence of which remain arguable.

Despite Descartes' best intentions, at the close of the *Meditations* all that is shown to be certain is that he or any other meditator can know that thought exists while thought is taking place. The dream hypothesis is never adequately rebutted, so strictly speaking sensory awareness remains problematic. Truths of reason remain equally problematic since the evil spirit may well survive to deceive us, since Descartes never rules out that God, though benevolent and not willing to deceive us, may tolerate a Satan who does deceive us, if only for the sake of challenging our faith, virtue, and ethical resolve.

In avoiding any suggestion that the evil spirit is Satan, Descartes effectively sidesteps the problem of evil. He manages to do so by focusing entirely on God's goodness and nondeceptiveness, thereby avoiding the question of how the occurrence of evil is compatible with divine goodness and limiting himself to consideration only of judgmental and perceptual error. Descartes almost certainly thinks that the answer to the problem of evil is that evil is our fault, as he argues in the fourth meditation regarding error. But even if we were to grant Descartes' point about error being our responsibility for judging hastily, that says nothing about illness, physical disasters, and other evils humans are subject to and which certainly cannot be attributed to hasty judgments.

* * *

The foregoing will strike readers as a very negative assessment of the *Meditations*, a work described earlier in this book as pivotal in the development of philosophy. Is the suggestion now that the *Meditations* should not be considered an important philosophical work? Not at all. The fact is that important philosophical works are sometimes, if not often, important precisely because they are misconceived or wrong, but are so in interesting and ultimately productive ways that prompt new ideas and useful reflection on old ones.

The *Meditations* are important if only because they constitute an intellectual distillate of epistemological and metaphysical notions and assumptions with long histories that needed to be forcefully and clearly stated before they could be properly assessed and rebutted or replaced with better ones.

The unfortunate part of the importance of wrong or misconceived philosophical works is that too many people are convinced by them and unreflectively accept their ill-thought presuppositions and objectives, and are swayed by their unsound arguments. This usually happens because people do not read critically enough – or reread often enough – to fully appreciate the implications of what they read.

The *Meditations* contain serious flaws. Descartes' presuppositions about the nature of mind and body, the absolute nature of truth, and the comprehensibility of perfection are highly problematic. His ready and uncritical recourse to the *ex nihilo* principle, his conception of existence as a property, and his acceptance of necessity as extending beyond propositions to events are just as questionable. However, Descartes' use of all of these in the *Meditations* did accomplish two things that have nothing to do with his own intentions. First, as just noted, the *Meditations* crystallized earlier philosophical thinking about the mind and body, knowledge, and God, thus enabling proper evaluation of what was for too long accepted as unproblematic. Second, the *Meditations* established epistemology as the dominant field of philosophy for some 300 years, displacing metaphysical speculation which had grown fruitless.

In this way, the *Meditations* left philosophy a significant legacy. A positive part of that legacy has to do with methodology: with the productive employment of skepticism and the need for rigor and critical thoroughness in philosophical thinking. The negative part of the legacy was the entrenching of two basic philosophical ideas that determined how Descartes' successors, particularly the British Empiricists and Kant, did philosophy: the issues they addressed, what they took for granted or as established, and what they thought needed doing. Descartes did not himself invent the two philosophical ideas central to the *Meditations*; Plato would have recognized both. But Descartes, 'the father of modern philosophy,' framed both ideas in forceful and imposing ways and gave them a currency that made both integral to Western philosophizing for quite a long time. The two ideas were that truth is absolute and ahistoric and that mind is substantial.

An interesting aspect of the dominance Descartes gave the ideas of truth as objective, in our contemporary sense, and of mind as substantial is that both ideas actually make being introduced to his work more challenging than it otherwise might be. While there is a great deal of material that is new to be learned and assimilated on first reading Descartes, these two ideas – truth's objectivity and the mind's substantiality – have filtered their way into ordinary thinking and are internalized by people in the process of being educated. Just think of the number of times you have heard references to truth conceived of as autonomous and independent of interests and events, and the number of references to the mind, not only as the persistent essence of what each of us is as a person over a lifetime, but as capable of surviving physical death.

What makes these two ideas oddly obstructive to the learning process when they are encountered in the *Meditations* is that they are encountered as familiar ideas, not as new ideas postulated in the arguments presented or entailed by those arguments. Readers then have the impression that they are reading about something familiar; they have the impression that Descartes is only saying some new things about truth and the mind rather than introducing particular and questionable conceptions of truth and of the mind. The result is that the *Meditations*' argument and contentions are more readily accepted than they should be. What we inherited from Descartes regarding truth and the mind is not always adequately reflected on, and sometimes is not even properly identified, which means that the *Meditations* often are not read critically enough when first encountered.

* * *

With respect to the idea of truth as objective, those of you reading this book and the *Meditations* in an academic context likely will be surprised at my saying that most contemporaries conceive of truth as objective. In academic circles, especially in the social-science disciplines, relativistic or what I describe in Chapter 1 as historicist conceptions of truth seem clearly dominant. However, this is an impression that is misleading in two different ways. First, many in the academic realm do still conceive of truth as objective and reject historicist or otherwise relativistic understandings of truth. If you have doubts about this, visit one of the science departments. But more important is the second way the impression is misleading, which is by presuming that those who endorse relativistic or historicist conceptions of truth do so in a reflective and well-grounded manner. This simply is not the case because far too many contemporaries, both academics and nonacademics, have compartmentalized and inherently inconsistent understandings of truth.

A large number of people accommodate our time's relativism or historicism and traditional objectivism regarding truth by thinking that objective truth is a rarely attained ideal and more generally understanding truth as relative or historical due to complexity and to perspectival limitations. The way this compartmentalization usually is expressed, and how it is normally thought justified, is by distinguishing between the 'hard' truths of the physical sciences and the 'soft' truths of the social sciences and of our complicated and diverse day-to-day interrelations with one another. Invariably there is recourse to the clarity of scientific contentions and the availability of applicable correctness-criteria to validate holding hard truths as objective, and to the lack of clarity and applicable criteria to validate holding soft truths as relative to ideological, social, and temporal contexts. Sometimes the compartmentalization is thought of or described as being pragmatic, as pragmatism, usually with little awareness or investigation of what pragmatism really is as a philosophical position.

With respect to the second troublesome aspect of our Cartesian inheritance, conception of the mind as substantial, things are as conceptually untidy as with truth. Most contemporaries appreciate – to a greater or lesser extent – that our consciousness is a highly complex product of neurophysiological processes and events. 'The mind,' however, is more than consciousness. It is a storehouse of information, of behavioral dispositions, of language and whatever enables language, of a great deal that is unconscious but nonetheless affects our moods and actions, and of much else that we do not yet understand. How all of this and our awareness and self-awareness are caused and sustained by neurophysiological processes is still not clear, despite how much we have learned. But more telling than lack of clarity regarding the physical causes of mentality is our experience: we, as conscious entities, do not experience our consciousness as a product of neurophysiological processes.

As with truth, then, there is recourse to compartmentalization. Regardless of how much we know about neurophysiology, most of us understand – and we all certainly experience – our selfhood and self-awareness as our being much closer to Descartes' thing-that-thinks than to the ephemeral products of firing synapses and other neural and physical goings-on. The consequence is that, for the most part, the mind is thought of as substantive despite what we know and readily admit about the dependency of the mental on the brain and central nervous system.

Ironically, in Cartesian terms, it is now more correct to say that the mind and thought are properties of the substance of extended matter rather than that the mind is an unextended substance defined by the property of thought. However, this changes nothing. Despite what we know, and the lip-service we pay materialistic understanding of the mind, most of us continue to think of the mind, of our minds – of ourselves – as Descartes portrays himself in the *Meditations*. And again, as a result the *Meditations* are not read critically enough.

*   *   *

Descartes' *Meditations on First Philosophy* are as vexing as they are inspiring; on the one hand, they offer arguments that do not work, on the other they serve as a model of sustained abstract thought. The *Meditations* are as philosophically obstructive as they were innovative; on the one hand they entrenched dubious views of truth and the mind, on the other they enabled more than three centuries of creative philosophizing. The *Meditations* are as regressive as they were stimulating; on the one hand they leapfrog backward to conceptions of truth and mind that essentially are those Plato held, on the other they prompt penetrating questions about the mind and truth.

For good or ill, the *Meditations* influenced philosophy in ways hugely out of proportion to their length, and did so in ways that while not what Descartes intended to achieve, nonetheless show that he was not far wrong in thinking his little book could make a great difference to human thought and knowledge. As should be clear, the most notable impact of Cartesian thought was epistemological. More specifically, Descartes determined how thousands of philosophers thought about our knowledge of the world and about truth. But things have changed. As indicated in Chapter 1 and above, many contemporaries reject Descartes' conception of truth as wholly objective – again, in our contemporary sense; not Descartes' sense of 'objective.' Many conceive of truth as relative, as historical, and are much more in the tradition of Protagoras and especially Nietzsche than that of Plato and Descartes (Krausz 1989).

The problem we face in proceeding is that dealing adequately with the issue of truth demands a great deal of exposition and discussion and is well beyond what I can attempt here. The best I can do, having indicated the nature of the debate, is to provide some good references. I strongly recommend that readers look at Barry Allen's *Truth in Philosophy*, Simon Blackburn's *Truth: A Guide*, and Bernard Williams' *Truth and Truthfulness* (Allen 1993; Blackburn 2005; Williams 2002). Though they deal with difficult questions and positions, all three books are surprisingly accessible and even those new to philosophy will gain from reading – and rereading – them. Of the three books, I think it best to start with Blackburn's, to continue with Williams', and then to read Allen's, the most inclusive of the three but also the most demanding.

With respect to saying something about Descartes' views and present-day philosophizing, particularly philosophizing as to whether we have or can achieve knowledge about the world, that is more manageable than trying to do justice to the issue of truth. The reason is that recent developments enable me to provide the essence of perhaps the most prominent aspect of the debate without requiring as much exposition and discussion as is required by the issue of truth.

CARTESIAN AND CONTEMPORARY PHILOSOPHY

Whatever else Descartes achieved, one thing he did not achieve was to conclusively resolve the issue he epitomized in his dream hypothesis, and so to establish as true his beliefs about external objects – including the existence of his own body. As a result, perhaps the major part of the Cartesian legacy is epistemological skepticism regarding knowledge of the material world, a skepticism the resolution of which in effect demands we do the impossible, namely, that we establish the veracity of our ideas' portrayal of their putative material causes while having no access to those causes except through those very ideas. This impossibility ultimately led to a contemporary philosophical – perhaps I should say 'ideological' – divergence that you need to know about in order to better retrospectively understand Descartes' thinking and its implications and how they relate to present-day philosophy.

The divergence in question is between thinking, on the one hand, that epistemological skepticism must be refuted, and thinking, on the other, that skepticism should be ignored. This is, in effect, a difference of opinion among philosophers as to whether the questions Descartes failed to answer need to be answered or were misconceived and should be forgotten. One contemporary philosopher referred to in Chapter 3, Davidson, believed that skepticism about our supposedly indirect access to the world must be countered and shown to be wrong. Another contemporary philosopher referred to in Chapter 2, Rorty, believed that the Cartesian basis for epistemology is seriously misconceived, hence unanswerable, and so has to be set aside.

In contrast to Peirce, who was mentioned in Chapter 1, and others who challenged Descartes on his own terms, Rorty, who until his death in 2007 was North America's leading postmodern philosopher, argued that Cartesian epistemological skepticism was a dead-end, the fruitless result of a wrongheaded understanding of mind and its contents, and that the questions it prompted, tried to answer, and saddled us with are an intellectual sham. Rorty characterized Descartes' misconceived understanding of mind as a representationalist view of awareness. The point of this characterization is that once we understand how Cartesian skepticism and the resulting epistemology are products of an inherently unworkable view of awareness of the world, we will dismiss both as not worth our time.

Rorty articulated the key notion of Cartesian thinking as a juxtaposition of us as conscious subjects to an autonomous and determinate physical world from which we, as aware entities, differ in kind. Then, because of our difference in kind from the physical world, it turns out that we have access to the world only through ideational facsimiles of it. That is, as wholly mental entities, as Descartes conceives us to be, we can be directly aware only of the contents of our own minds, so we can be aware of the world solely through the ideational representations of the world which occur in our minds. What follows from this juxtaposition is the ultimately hopeless epistemological project of trying to verify that the ideational representations in our minds are accurate representations of a world we can know only through those putative representations. The hopelessness of this task is why in the sixth meditation Descartes has to resort to our convictions and to God's goodness and nondeceptive nature to guarantee those convictions.

What is important to appreciate here is that Rorty's challenge to Cartesian epistemology is not a move within epistemology; it is an attempt to undermine epistemology by revealing how it arises from deep misconception. In short, Rorty refuses to play Descartes' game, preferring to abandon the game altogether. This brings me to a point that may strike you as overly subtle but which is nonetheless important.

When Descartes failed to conclusively prove the existence of extended matter, the question of matter's existence became the broader question of whether the ideas that present themselves to us as representations of things independent of our minds – that is, as things not imagined or otherwise produced by us – can be deemed to actually be representations of things external to our minds. If so, then matter exists – with or without divine guarantees. But the key point is that there can be ideas – or images or sensory effects – in the mind or available to the mind which have causes or origins outside the mind. Initially it may appear that establishing that this is the case answers Descartes' questions, but the point here is that it does not, because it leaves open the question of how faithful what is in the mind is to what is outside the mind. This question, or just the possibility of it arising, is what Rorty sees as the core of Cartesian misconceived representationalism.

Rorty uses the metaphor of mirroring to elucidate the Cartesian conception. He attributes Cartesian epistemological concerns to a view of the mind as 'a mirror of nature' (Rorty 1979). His point is that in the Cartesian conception, the aware mind portrays the world by producing ideational representations of it, hence the possibility – or need – of asking if it does so accurately.

Locke made representationalism worse by adding grist to the mill regarding how representations in the mind may differ from the external causes they supposedly portray. More or less building on Descartes' concern that properties such as color inhere in the representations and not their causes, Locke contributed the notion that there is a difference between 'primary qualities,' or properties which characterize the things in the world in themselves, and 'secondary qualities,' or properties which are features of our experience of the world. Berkeley complicated things further by arguing that primary properties were at best redundant and at worst chimerical and attempting to reduce all properties to mental properties. Hume, of course, drew the obvious and inevitable conclusion and embraced the impossibility of the epistemological task by reducing everything to impressions and ideas, acknowledging only a difference of degree of vivacity between impressions and ideas, but in doing so Hume basically brought epistemology to a dead end. For his part, Kant added to the mirror idea by arguing that however the world may be in itself, though we can know it, we can know it only within the confines of certain modes of awareness that organize and shape the world's effects on us into coherent, graspable experience.

The distinction Kant drew was between a world unknowable in itself and how we represent that world's effects on us to ourselves. Difficult though it is for some to accept or even to fully understand, Kant included the most basic properties we experience, such as temporality, spatiality and causality, in how we represent the world to ourselves. That is, even time, space, and causal connection are modes of how we represent the world rather than being elements of the world. As for how the world may be in itself, without the intercession of conceptualization, that is something which is literally unthinkable.

Kant's enhancement of the original Cartesian representationalist conception, his making our subjectivity a more active one in giving the mind a configuring role in awareness, really changed nothing. The basic idea was still that we may know something about what is 'out there' only by having replicas 'in here.' In fact, in a way Kant's enhancement made things worse because it enabled the possibility that different subjects might configure the world differently in undetectably diverse ways. This meant there could be as many experienced worlds as there are subjects of experience. The mirror-of-nature conception of awareness and knowledge grew more complex and difficult – albeit more interesting – as more philosophers contributed to the debate, but the conception did not get better.

* * *

Generally, the problem with Cartesian representationalism that Rorty is concerned to highlight is that once awareness is understood as mediated by representations, we are isolated as subjects by an unbridgeable gulf which opens between us and the world. We become isolated nonextended points of awareness while the world becomes an inaccessible mystery of which we have only second-hand cognizance.

Rorty thought that the central problem with Cartesian thinking in general, and Descartes' epistemological project in particular, is that the mind is thought of as internally portraying the world to itself, with all that is entailed by the internal/external distinction. Rorty tells us that if we have 'a simple theory of the . . . mind either getting, or failing to get, a clear view of [external] things,' then we will naturally think that 'inquiry consists in getting our "representations" into shape, rather than simply describing the world' (Rorty 1982, 15). In addition, we will take it that what we must first do when we philosophize is not try to say how things are, but rather try to establish that we can know how things are by testing our internal representations with skeptical devices such as the dream hypothesis. Differently put, what would otherwise be taken as knowledge of the world is taken to be a complex facsimile and so only potentially a correct portrait of the world.

Rorty argued that once we accept the Cartesian epistemological structure, once we accept that consciousness is essentially the having of representations of external reality, then not only is Descartes' project of trying to prove those representations accurate an inevitable one, but it is also an unachievable one. As has been made clear earlier, the very premise that generates the project precludes its successful conclusion. If our awareness of the world must always be indirect, through representations, we can never really know that the representations are faithful to the world.

How, you may be wondering, could Descartes have had so much influence if his thinking was so misguided? And if it was so misguided, why is it important to learn about it and understand it? These are questions that tend to separate those with a bent for philosophy from those less interested. However, the answers to both questions are forceful and convincing only to some. The answer to the second question has two parts: if you want to understand philosophy now, you need to understand what it once was and how it got to be what it is; and if you want to do philosophy, you need to understand where and how it has gone wrong before.

The answer to the first question is a bit more difficult to articulate succinctly; essentially it is that the traditions and the presuppositions and assumptions current at any point in historical time have a huge influence on people's thinking. As you will have learned in working through the foregoing chapters and the *Meditations*, despite his efforts at thoroughgoing critical assessment of everything he believed, Descartes unreflectively accepted a great deal current in his intellectual milieu – for instance, the *ex nihilo* principle, the Aristotelian conception of substance. And as you were warned early in this book, elements in your intellectual milieu, particularly historicist or relativistic views of truth, could easily influence your reading of the *Meditations*. No one philosophizes in a vacuum, and no one's philosophy is learned and assimilated in a vacuum. Much of Descartes' influence was a function of what was going on in his time, and that influence grew as his work shaped the intellectual milieu of his successors.

* * *

I close this part of the chapter with a brief observation regarding the thorny issue of truth. There is an implication to be drawn from the conception of ourselves as isolated consciousnesses in touch with reality only through representations. The implication is that as Descartes and those who followed in the tradition he established assumed, truth must be autonomous and objective for there to be knowledge. The reason is that the 'fit' between our veridical ideas and the world cannot be merely a matter of perspective, for that may vary and might be distorted or otherwise idiosyncratic.

On the Cartesian scheme, knowledge can only be knowledge if the fit of ideas to their causes is guaranteed by something other than our own beliefs and interpretations. There must be objective truth if there is to be knowledge; our ideas must conform to their causes in a way wholly independent of ourselves, a way that conforms to standards wholly independent of us, else we would all wind up in distinct universes where what is the case just is whatever we take to be the case. Despite the fact that Descartes began by holding truth as ahistoric, as absolute, as wholly objective, he would have to have accepted truth as objective (in our sense) because of his conception of the mind and awareness of the world. Had he even considered the possibility, Descartes did not have the option to hold truth historical or relative.

In the end, the *Meditations* leave us less philosophically secure than we were before their advent. It is not that we had certainty before Descartes and lost it when he raised his questions; it is rather that his questions enabled a number of epistemological positions that had not been articulated in ways forceful enough to determine the course of philosophy for centuries. Early Greek skeptics explored the possibility that knowledge of the world is unattainable, but they came nowhere near Descartes' success in influencing successors. Understanding the *Meditations*, then, is something you need to do if you have any interest in philosophy: starting with Descartes is starting with his *Meditations*.

BIOGRAPHICAL SKETCH

I end this book with a brief account of points in Descartes' relatively short life that are of greatest relevance to forming an impression of the man behind the philosophy.

Descartes was born at La Haye, near Tours, France, on March 31, 1596. His formative years were spent under the tutelage of Jesuits at their La Flèche College in Anjou. It is unclear just how long Descartes was at La Flèche; he may have been admitted as early as 1604, when he was 8 years old, or as late as 1606, when he was ten. He was there eight or possibly 10 years, leaving in 1614, but he was certainly at La Flèche long enough to have been significantly influenced by Jesuit teaching and discipline. In 1616, Descartes took a *Baccalauréat* and a *Licence* in law at the University of Poitiers, achievements that at that time immediately put him in a small minority and which provided the basic credentials for his later intellectual efforts.

Likely against familial expectations, Descartes went to Holland in 1618, just 2 years after finishing at Poitiers. Even more likely against expectations, he joined the army of Prince Maurice of Nassau (Maurice of Orange). However, 1618 also saw the beginnings of his intellectual pursuits and the blossoming of his originality. In that year he wrote his *Compendium Musicae*, though it remained unpublished.

The next year, 1619, Descartes traveled in Germany and in that year he apparently had a number of insights regarding mathematics. However, rather than pursue those insights in an academic context, as he might well have done, he returned to France and spent the next few years in Paris, seemingly content to discuss his ideas with others of like mind and making occasional brief trips to other European countries. In 1620, he wrote *Cogitationes Privatae*, though that work also remained unpublished.

It was in 1628 that Descartes wrote his *Rules for the Direction of the Mind*, basically his first work with significant philosophical implications and decidedly a harbinger of what he was to produce in the next dozen years, and this despite the work not being completed or published. Also in 1628 he returned to Holland, where he would remain for the next 21 years of his life. There is little question that the intellectual and ideologically more liberal environment Holland provided was considerably more conducive to Descartes' productivity than that which he found in France. In 1629, he began to write *The World*, something he might well not have attempted in France. In this period he also wrote all or much of his *Treatise on Man*. However, in 1633 he decided not to pursue or publish either work because of the ecclesiastical condemnation of Galileo's helio-centric contentions. It merits mention at this point that Descartes' works going unpublished did not mean they went unread. At the time there was a healthy exchange of views among intellectuals and what Descartes wrote was no doubt read by many despite not being published.

The year 1635 saw the birth of Descartes' short-lived daughter – as far as we know his only child. The daughter was born out of wedlock and she died in 1640, when she was barely 5 years old. Descartes' father died the same year. There is no adequate basis on which to ground any conclusions about how the birth and early death of his daughter or the death of his father may have affected Descartes or whether, in fact, these events had much impact on him.

1637 was a productive year. Descartes published his first cen-trally philosophical work, the *Discourse on Method*, as well as his *Dioptrics, Geometry* and *Meteorology*. These were Descartes' first published works.

The *Meditations on First Philosophy* followed fairly quickly, in 1641. The *Meditations*, considerably more widely read and com-mented on than his other books, were first published together with six sets of objections and replies. In 1642, just one year later, a second edition of the *Meditations* was published, this time with seven sets of objections and replies and with the *Letter to Dinet*.

In 1643, a decade after the furor over Galileo, Descartes had happened to meet what he had feared and avoided since Galileo's trial: Descartes' philosophical views were publicly condemned at the University of Utrecht – a significant center of learning and, one might add, ideological and religious orthodoxy. It was precisely to avoid this sort of condemnation that Descartes earlier refrained from publishing *The World*.

Perhaps partly to take advantage of a highly placed sympathetic ear, it was also in 1643 that Descartes began his long correspondence with Bohemia's Princess Elizabeth, someone who was receptive to his ideas and who prompted Descartes to elucidate much of what he had written by raising stimulating and perceptive questions about his claims and pronouncements. Some of Descartes' letters to Princess Elizabeth are of special interest to anyone who is puzzled or intrigued by his metaphysical distinction between mind and body (Kenny 1970).

In 1644, Descartes again visited France, and it was also in 1644 that he published his *Principles of Philosophy*.

No doubt because of the intellectual reputation he had achieved by that time, and the significantly widespread response to his writings, particularly to the *Meditations*, Descartes was granted a pension in 1647 by the French king, Louis XIV – or the appropriate minion, since Louis XIV was only nine in 1647. It is unlikely that Descartes had real need of the pension, but he certainly would have welcomed it as recognition in his native country of the status his works had won for him.

In 1649 Descartes published *The Passions of the Soul*. Another notable but much less fortunate event that occurred in 1649 was that Descartes undertook his ill-fated trip to Sweden at the invitation of Queen Christina.

The Queen seems to have had a serious interest in philosophy, but the story goes that she insisted on discussing philosophy with Descartes at or before daybreak, a practice that apparently was very hard on Descartes. Likely due to his inability to adapt to the harsh Swedish weather, a problem exacerbated by what he seems to have found a fatiguing schedule imposed on him by the Queen's expectations, Descartes apparently contracted pneumonia. The illness proved fatal, possibly because of related complications. He was only 54 when he died in Stockholm in 1650, a mere year after accepting Queen Christina's invitation.

SELECT BIBLIOGRAPHY

Because this is an introductory text, I have deliberately kept the Bibliography as brief as possible. It contains only works cited and a few others that readers new to Descartes and philosophy should find of interest. Six entries are marked as 'must read' or 'must have' because of their excellence and special importance to understanding and appreciating Descartes' work in particular and philosophy in general.

Allen, Barry (1993). *Truth in Philosophy*. Cambridge, MA: Harvard University Press.

Audi, Robert (1996). *The Cambridge Dictionary of Philosophy*. Cambridge: Cambridge University Press, 193–196. (This is a 'must have' for anyone interested in philosophy.)

Blackburn, Simon (2005). *Truth: A Guide*. Oxford: Oxford University Press. (Another 'must have' book, if only for its reference value.)

Cornford, Francis (1957). *Plato's Theory of Knowledge*. New York: Bobbs-Merrill.

Cottingham, John, ed. and trans. (1995). *René Descartes: Meditations on First Philosophy, with Selections from the Objections and Replies*. Cambridge: Cambridge University Press.

Cottingham, John, Robert Stoothoff and Dugald Murdoch (1985). *The Philosophical Writings of Descartes*. Cambridge: Cambridge University Press.

Davidson, Donald (1986). 'A Coherence Theory of Truth and Knowledge.' In Ernest LePore, ed., *Truth and Interpretation: Perspectives on the Philosophy of Donald Davidson*. New York: Blackwell, 307–39.

Debus, Allen G. (1978). *Man and Nature in the Renaissance*. Cambridge: Cambridge University Press.

Descartes, René. *Meditations on First Philosophy*. Laurence J. Lafleur, trans., Macmillan/Library of Liberal Arts, 1951 (1989); also Haldane and Ross, 1969.

—— *Meditations on First Philosophy*. Cottingham, 1995.

—— *Discourse on Method*. Haldane and Ross, 1969.

—— *Arguments*. Haldane and Ross, 1969.

—— *Reply to Objections IV*. Haldane and Ross, 1969.

Foucault, Michel (1973). *The Order of Things*. New York: Vintage.

—— (1980). *Power/Knowledge: Selected Interviews and Other Writings*. ed. Colin Gordon. New York: Pantheon.

—— (1986). *The Use of Pleasure*. trans. Robert Hurley. New York: Vintage.

—— (1989). *Foucault Live*. Sylvère Lotringer, ed., and trans. John Johnston. New York: Semiotext(e).

Fox-Keller, Evelyn (1985). *Reflections on Gender and Science*. New Haven: Yale University Press.

Haldane, Elizabeth, and G. R. T. Ross (1969). *The Philosophical Works of Descartes* (Volumes I and II). Cambridge: Cambridge University Press.

Honderich, Ted, ed. (1995). *The Oxford Companion to Philosophy*. Oxford and New York: Oxford University Press, 188–192. (This is a 'must read' book.)

Kemp-Smith, Norman (1958). *Descartes: Philosophical Writings*. New York: The Modern Library/Random House.

Kenny, Anthony, trans. and ed. (1970). *Descartes: Philosophical Letters*. Oxford: Clarendon Press.

Kiernan, Thomas P. (1962). *Aristotle Dictionary*. New York: Philosophical Library.

Krausz, Michael (1989). *Relativism: Interpretation and Confrontation*. Notre Dame, Ind.: Notre Dame University Press.

Matson, Wallace I. (1965). *The Existence of God*. Ithaca: Cornell University Press.

—— (2000). *A New History of Philosophy* (Second edition, Volumes 1 and 2). New York: Harcourt. (Matson's history is another 'must read' for anyone learning about or doing philosophy.)

Morris, John M. (1971). *Descartes Dictionary*. New York: Philosophical Library. (Though now somewhat difficult to find, this is another 'must read' book regarding Descartes.)

Nietzsche, Friedrich Wilhelm (1968a). *The Will to Power*. Walter Kaufman, ed., trans. Kaufman and R. J. Hollingdale. New York: Vintage Books.

—— (1968b). *Thus Spoke Zarathustra*. In Walter Kaufman (1968), *The Portable Nietzsche*. New York: Penguin.

O'Farrell, Clare (1989). *Foucault: Historian or Philosopher?* Houndmills: Macmillan.

Prado, C. G. (2000). *Starting with Foucault: An Introduction to Genealogy*, Second Edition. Boulder, Colo. and San Francisco: Westview Press.

—— , ed. (2003). *A House Divided: Comparing Analytic and Continental Philosophy*. Amherst, New York: Humanity Books (Prometheus).

Rorty, Richard (1979). *Philosophy and the Mirror of Nature*. Princeton: Princeton University Press.

—— (1982). *The Consequences of Pragmatism*. Minneapolis: University of Minnesota Press.

Searle, John (1999). *Mind, Language and Society*. London: Phoenix.

Sellars, Wilfrid (1962). 'Philosophy and the Scientific Image of Man.' In Robert Colodny, ed., *Frontiers of Science and Philosophy*. Pittsburgh, PA: University of Pittsburgh.

Snow, Charles Percy (1959). *Two Cultures*. Cambridge: Cambridge University Press.

Williams, Bernard (2002). *Truth and Truthfulness*. Princeton: Princeton University Press.

—— (2005). *Descartes: The Project of Pure Enquiry*. London and New York: Routledge. (A 'must have' book for those interested in Descartes.)

Wilson, Margaret (1978). *Descartes*. New York: Routledge.

GLOSSARY

The following entries are provided to help you understand the technical terms used in the text. The entries are not intended to provide definitive definitions. For more extensive coverage of the terms listed, you should use a good dictionary of philosophy. The one I recommend is Robert Audi's *The Cambridge Dictionary of Philosophy*. (See Select Bibliography.)

ANALYTIC: Said of an expression the truth of which depends only on the meaning of the terms used. In Kantian terms, these expressions are described as ones where the subject 'contains' the predicate in the sense that all we need to do to establish the truth of the expression is analyze the sense of the subject. Examples range from evident identity statements such as 'A is A' to statements like 'All bachelors are unmarried men.'

ANTI-EPISTEMOLOGY, ANTI-EPISTEMOLOGIST: see EPISTEMOLOGY.

BEHAVIORISM: The view that our talk about minds is exhaustively reducible to talk about verbal or bodily behavior.

CLARITY, DISTINCTNESS: Descartes' qualifiers for ideas that present themselves to the mind in a perfectly transparent way, i.e., involving no confusion or ambiguity, and wholly contained in themselves and not as dependent on other ideas.

CONCEPT: Essentially a recognitional capacity. Having the concept of red means being able to pick out something of a certain sort: i.e., something red. Often 'concept' is wrongly used as synonymous with 'idea.' In philosophy, 'concept' is used mainly to designate intellectual recognitional capacities, such as having the capacity to understand description of an act as a moral act.

CONSTRUCTIVIST: One who believes that the objects of human

knowledge are, at least in part and at least as present to us, determined by historical and psychological factors and so are conditioned by subjective elements belonging to their mode of apprehension.

DECONSTRUCTION: This term is too widely used at present to allow for rigid definition. Basically it refers to the sort of critique practiced by Jacques Derrida which involves teasing out from any given position elements antithetical to that same position. Effectively the objective is to show any and all positions to be no more than favored perspectives.

DETERMINISM: The view that everything that occurs is brought about by a sufficient cause and hence could not have been otherwise.

DISTINCTNESS: See CLARITY.

DUALISM: The view that there are two fundamentally different substances: mind or the mental and body or the material. This view differentiates so totally between mind and body, between the mental and the physical, that it raises serious issues about how the mind and body can and do interact. Most of Descartes' rationalist successors endorsed mind/body dualism.

EMPIRICISM: Basically the philosophical position that all knowledge derives from experience. Empiricism is best understood as the denial of the basic tenet of Rationalism, namely, that there is some knowledge that derives from reason alone and which is independent of experience.

EPISTEMOLOGY: The theory of knowledge, which inquires into what can be known, with what degree of certainty and under what conditions; that central area of philosophy concerned with the nature and justification of knowledge claims. Epistemologists are concerned to 'ground' human knowledge in either self-verifying truths or an experiential 'given.' An anti-epistemologist is one who believes that human knowledge cannot be justified beyond consensus, general effectiveness or pragmatic value, and practice.

ETHICS: That part of value-theory which includes aesthetics, having to do with the study of the nature and justification of judgments about right and wrong conduct. Note that in our culture ethics is often confused with the religious, or at least seen as entailing or being entailed by the religious. While religious views invariably entail or involve ethical views, the reverse is not the case, in spite of the common view. One need not be religious to be ethical, and an ethic or moral code can be quite independent of any religious notion. 'Ethics' and 'ethical' are usually used synonymously with 'morality' and 'moral.' Some use 'ethics' and 'ethical' to refer to what is universally correct with respect to conduct, and 'morality' and 'moral' to refer to what a particular culture considers to be ethical.

EXISTENTIALISM: The position, most notably that of Jean-Paul Sartre, which maintains that existence precedes essence. In other words, it is a denial of essences and an affirmation of the constitutive role of practice and the responsibility of the individual for self-determination. Usually existentialism is maintained as an ethical position. A looser, more popular sense is that having to do with the isolation of the individual and the individual's confrontation of pressing but ambiguous situations.

INTUITION: Though Kant's use of 'intuition' is more like our use of 'sense' or even 'experience', earlier philosophers like Descartes used 'intuition' to refer to direct awareness of truth without need of inferences or analysis. Usually, in philosophy, 'intuition' is used with respect to claimed direct awareness of ethical value.

METAPHYSICAL: That which pertains to metaphysics, as in 'metaphysical claim' or 'metaphysical element'. See METAPHYSICS.

METAPHYSICS: That part of philosophical inquiry and speculation that concerns itself with ultimate reality and the fundamental nature of what exists, as well as with what can exist. See ONTOLOGY.

METHODOLOGICAL DOUBT: Doubt assumed for the purpose of proving whatever is doubted, a device used to strategically impugn what might otherwise not be questioned. Though methodological doubt is taken seriously in application, it does not entail or require that what is under examination, a belief, say, actually is or must be thought false.

METHODOLOGY: A rule-governed procedure or set of procedures for dealing with a problematic matter.

OBJECTIVIST: One who believes the objects of knowledge to be free of subjective components contributed by the knower and so not conditioned by psychological or historical factors or other elements having to do with their apprehension or mode of apprehension.

ONTOLOGY, ONTOLOGICAL: the subdiscipline in philosophy which deals with being as such: with what is and what can be. Ontological questions are about the ultimate and/or relative nature of the subjects of discourse: minds, material objects, and experiences.

A POSTERIORI: That which is learned from experience and cannot be known prior to or without experience of the world.

POSTMODERN, POSTMODERNIST: While the term 'postmodern' originally applied to art, it is now used to mean intellectual methods, objectives, values, topics, and interests which share rejection of the Enlightenment assumption of the existence and discernibility of objective truth and the possibility of real, cumulative progress in inquiry. A somewhat looser sense of 'postmodern,' but one common in present-day philosophy, focuses on denial of the objectivity of truth. A postmodernist is one who espouses postmodernism.

PRIMARY QUALITY: Supposedly, the qualities or properties objects in the world actually have in the sense of not being perception-dependent, such as their mass, size, figure, and number. See SECONDARY QUALITY.

A PRIORI: That which can be known prior to or without the need of experience. For example, it is *a priori* that the internal angles of a triangle equal 180 degrees. One does not need to go about measuring triangles to know this is true. Note that empiricists identify the *a priori* and the analytic (see ANALYTIC), while rationalists think them different. In other words, empiricists think that analytic expressions are necessarily true by definition. Rationalists believe some may be true or false in ways not dependent on definitions – for instance, because of the necessity of a mode of representation.

PROPOSITION: For some, simply a thought, or the content of a thought; that which can be thought or articulated in a spoken or written sentence. The proposition is what is translated from, say, an English sentence to a French sentence. The proposition is what is true or false. The proposition is what is said in a sentence, so: 'The sentence "The cat is sleeping" says the same as the Spanish sentence "El gato duerme."' With respect to belief, the proposition is what is believed. Some use 'proposition' more or less synonymously with 'sentence.'

RATIONAL: That which is properly reasoned; also that which satisfies criteria having to do with logical validity. The common sense in which we speak of someone being 'rational,' as opposed to mad or deranged, derives from the philosophical sense that what distinguishes us as human beings is that we reason as opposed to only respond to stimuli or emotional prompts.

RATIONALISM: The philosophical position that at least some knowledge derives from reason alone. As with EMPIRICISM, this position is best understood in terms of its opposite: that is, as the stance opposing the claim that knowledge derives solely from experience.

REASON: Narrowly, our ability to establish and implement suitable means-to-ends measures to attain our goals; more broadly, the ability to think coherently and to think reflectively or in a self-aware mode.

RELATIVISM: The view that because there are no objective standards or determinants, truth- and value-judgments are always relative to cultural, group, or personal preferences. This is sometimes put provocatively as the view that any position or claim is as good as any other.

SECONDARY QUALITY: Supposedly a quality or property attributed to an object only because of the action of that object on a percipient: specifically, taste, color, odor, feel, and sound.

SELF-EVIDENT: That the truth (or falsity) of which is present in the very thought of it, as in the self-evidency of the truth of 'A=A' or the self-evident falsity of 'squared circle.' Usually 'self-evident' is applied to principles, such as the principle of noncontradiction.

SENSES: Our sensory apparatus. More importantly, knowledge acquired through the senses is usually contrasted, in philosophy, with knowledge acquired through intuition or rational inference or claimed to be part and parcel of being rational.

SOLIPSISM: The view that nothing exists except for what is immediately given to consciousness – it follows from solipsism that there are no other consciousnesses but that of the solipsist, since no one can experience another's consciousness. There are solipsistic implications in a number of Descartes' contentions, and they are serious in direct proportion to his inadequacies in his proofs of God's existence and of the existence of the external world. Note that few philosophers endorse solipsism; usually it is used as a charge against a philosophical position.

SUBSTANCE: That which exists independently of all else – as opposed to a property, which must inhere in a substance or substantial thing.

SUFFICIENT CAUSE/SUFFICIENT CONDITION: Usually contrasted with necessary cause/condition. A sufficient cause/condition is or would be all that is or would be needed for something to happen: it is sufficient that the powder in a shell explode for the bullet to be fired, while it is a necessary but not sufficient cause/condition of the bullet's being fired that the powder be dry.

SYNTHETIC: Said of sentences, propositions or judgments, and usually defined in Kant's terms as a sentence, proposition, or judgment in which the predicate adds new information to the subject. In practice, synthetic sentences, propositions, and judgments are experience-based, as opposed to analytic ones, where the predicate is said to be 'contained' in the subject and hence adds no new information to what is understood about the subject. Analytic sentences, propositions, and judgments are true or false on the basis of definition or, as some contend, on the basis of meaning. Against this, synthetic ones are true or false on the basis of how we discern the world to be.

THEOLOGY: That part of human inquiry concerned with determining, to the best extent possible, the nature of God.

TRUTH: This is a tough one, because the main issue is whether truth admits of definition, and if so, of what sort of theoretical definition: for example, as the 'correspondence' of sentences to facts ('Correspondence theory'), or as the 'coherence' among sentences ('Coherence theory'). The contemporary critics of Cartesian philosophizing insist that truth does not admit of theoretical definition, and that to call a sentence 'true' is only to make a certain kind of endorsement in language. For discussion of Descartes' views, take 'truth' to be correspondence of sentences to facts or to 'how the world is.'

VERIFICATION: As used in philosophy, the establishing of the truth or falsity of some claim or belief by appealing to actual or at least possible sense experience. 'Verificationism' is, roughly, the view that for claims to be meaningful they must be confirmable by actual or possible experience.

Verificationists oppose metaphysical speculation, claiming that anything not verifiable by experience is literally meaningless and at most an emotive expression of a complex sort.

INDEX